Praise for
Happily Ever After...and 39 Other Myths about Love

"You'll do more than enjoy reading these hope-filled vignettes of couples who were able to discern and overcome the unconscious myth that blocked their loving connection. You'll likely also discern the myth that blocks happiness in your own relationship."

— Sylvia Boorstein, PhD, author of *Happiness Is an Inside Job*

"Busting myths about marriage and other intimate partnerships is a creative way to present and promote clear thinking. In their book *Happily Ever After*, the Blooms have drawn on research, literature, and their own challenging experiences to bring to readers succinct, impactful, and wise truths that dispel the myths that have plagued popular thinking about intimate relationships. And all in one place! Every couple will become wiser by reading this book, and their skills will be better honed by practicing those recommended here."

— Harville Hendrix, PhD, coauthor (with Helen LaKelly Hunt, PhD) of
Making Marriage Simple: Ten Relationship-Saving Truths

"In *Happily Ever After*, Linda and Charlie Bloom deconstruct the most common myths about love and commitment in a thoughtful and compassionate way. The Blooms deeply understand the obstacles that hold people back from lasting love and provide readers with sensible workarounds to each of these obstacles. This book will challenge some of your most deeply held beliefs about love and marriage, ultimately freeing you to make better choices in love."

— Kira Asatryan, author of *Stop Being Lonely:*
Three Simple Steps to Developing Close Friendships and Deep Relationships

"Bravo to the Blooms for providing this important clue for removing the invisible roadblocks that prevent relationships from flourishing."

— Seymour Boorstein, MD, author of
Who's Talking Now: Saving Your Relationship

"We applaud Linda and Charlie Bloom for their conciseness, skill, and dedication to myth busting. If you want an authentic relationship, read this book!"

— Joyce Vissell, RN, MS, and Barry Vissell, MD,
The Shared Heart

"By dispelling these forty relationship-killing myths, the Blooms have cleared yet another path to cultivate the kind of intimacy that leads to true happiness. *Happily Ever After* is sure to become a standard for anyone seeking the better version of themselves and their relationship."

— Dr. Ken Druck, author of
The Real Rules of Life: Balancing Life's Terms with Your Own

"*Happily Ever After...and 39 Other Myths about Love* courageously turns false beliefs fostered by fairy tales and romance novels on their head. In real life, happy couples can argue, continue appreciating each other over time, and heal from old wounds — if they think of marriage not as a fixed destination but as a process to which they commit. Authors Linda and Charlie Bloom encourage us not necessarily to discard the myths but to consider taking on a different point of view. This book is a wise, sensitive guide for anyone committed to keeping a relationship thriving."

— Marcia Naomi Berger, MSW, LCSW,
author of *Marriage Meetings for Lasting Love*

"Linda and Charlie Bloom's eye-opening new book is a marvelous deconstruction of the illusions and sometimes outright fallacies that undermine healthy and nurturing relationships, illuminating the gap between how we imagine love to be and how it actually is and can be. Their faith in the possibility of soul-satisfying relationships is moving in itself. This is a rubber-meets-the-road guide to preparing for the rigors (and rewards) of love. High five to the Blooms for telling it like it is."

— Gregg Levoy, author of *Vital Signs: Discovering and Sustaining Your Passion for Life* and *Callings: Finding and Following an Authentic Life*

"As in their bestseller, *101 Things I Wish I Knew When I Got Married*, Linda and Charlie Bloom bring compassionate insight and the hard-won savvy derived from their own enduring veteran marriage to *Happily Ever After...and 39 Other Myths about Love*. This is a book about the chasm between rigidly held beliefs and authentic experience, about what is possible in relationships when partners are willing to suspend conventional 'wisdom' and clichéd sentiment. It is in many ways a survival manual for the committed couple."

— David Kerns, MD, retired Stanford medical professor and author of
Standard of Care and the forthcoming *Fortnight on Maxwell Street*

"Long-term relationships are more challenging than ever. *Happily Ever After...and 39 Other Myths about Love*, like the Blooms' previous books, is filled with gems of relationship wisdom to help make the journey joyful and deeper over time. They offer readers of all ages valuable guidelines and tools that are certain to enhance their ability to create lasting and fulfilling relationships."

— Ken and Maddy Dychtwald, cofounders of Age Wave

"*Happily Ever After* is a true myth buster. Linda and Charlie Bloom skillfully challenge, one by one, relationship myths that do more damage than good. Their grounded, compassionate, and effective approach to creating great relationships will prove an essential guide for many people who sincerely seek a sustainable, loving relationship."

— Judith Bell, MS, and Daniel Ellenberg, PhD,
Rewire Leadership Institute, authors of *Lovers for Life*

"Linda and Charlie Bloom have written a fantastic book! It is wise, honest, personal, and deeply engaging. They have dispelled the cultural myths about love that cause the most trouble and replaced them with wise and honestly earned truths. This much-needed book is recommended for singles and couples alike."

— Linda Carroll, author of
Love Cycles: The Five Essential Stages of Lasting Love

"The Blooms' latest book, *Happily Ever After...and 39 Other Myths about Love*, is another brilliant contribution by this remarkable couple to everyone struggling to create a relationship that works. The book acknowledges some of the biggest pitfalls couples fall into when they fail to challenge the conventional thinking about relationships. The authors call into question these all-too-common cultural beliefs and, more importantly, offer compelling ways to avoid being possessed by them. This is a book about freedom — about transformation — and it's a must-read for anyone seeking to create a truly fulfilling partnership!"

— Lynne Twist, author of *The Soul of Money*

Happily Ever After...
and 39 Other Myths
about Love

Also by Linda and Charlie Bloom

101 Things I Wish I Knew When I Got Married

Secrets of Great Marriages

Happily Ever After... and 39 Other Myths about Love

Breaking Through to the Relationship of Your Dreams

Linda & Charlie Bloom

New World Library
Novato, California

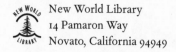

New World Library
14 Pamaron Way
Novato, California 94949

Text design by Megan Colman

Library of Congress Cataloging-in-Publication Data
Names: Bloom, Linda, date. | Bloom, Charlie, date.
Title: Happily ever after...and 39 other myths about love : breaking through to the relationship of your dreams / Linda and Charlie Bloom.
Description: Novato, California : New World Library, [2016]
Identifiers: LCCN 2015050045 | ISBN 9781608683949 (paperback)
Subjects: LCSH: Marriage.|Man-woman relationships. | Interpersonal relations. | Love. | BISAC: FAMILY & RELATIONSHIPS / Marriage. | FAMILY & RELATIONSHIPS / Love & Romance.
Classification: LCC HQ734 .B65734 2016 | DDC 306.81—dc23
LC record available at http://lccn.loc.gov/2015050045

First printing, April 2016
ISBN 978-1-60868-394-9
EISBN 978-1-60868-395-6
Printed in Canada on 100% postconsumer-waste recycled paper

10   9   8   7   6   5   4   3   2   1

Contents

Foreword by Susan Campbell   xiii

Introduction   xvii

Myth 1 And they lived happily ever after.   1

Myth 2 People expect too much from relationships.   6

Myth 3 If we fight, it means we're not meant for each other.   11

Myth 4 A happy childhood is a prerequisite
        to a great relationship.   16

Myth 5 Marriages inevitably get flat, stale,
        and boring over time.   21

Myth 6 Once a cheater, always a cheater.   24

Myth 7 All you need is love.   29

Myth 8 When you've lost that loving feeling,
        it's gone, gone, gone.   33

Myth 9 All differences need to be reconciled.   38

Myth 10   Time heals all wounds.   41

Myth 11   You need to disclose all your past experiences
in order to build trust.   45

Myth 12   Commitment and freedom are mutually exclusive.   48

Myth 13   Little things aren't worth getting upset about.   52

Myth 14   Relationships shouldn't have to be this hard.   55

Myth 15   All the good men/women are taken.   59

Myth 16   Nothing good can come from conflict.   62

Myth 17   True lovers feel love for each other all the time.   65

Myth 18   If you really loved me, I wouldn't have to ask.   71

Myth 19   Love will heal my past emotional pain.   76

Myth 20   You can be right and have a good relationship.   81

Myth 21   After I'm married, I won't ever be lonely again.   84

Myth 22   Commitment means staying together no matter what.   88

Myth 23   Telling the truth means getting it all off your chest.   92

Myth 24   Love means never having to say you're sorry.   98

Myth 25   There's just not enough time.   102

Myth 26   When it comes to togetherness in relationships,
more is always better.   107

Myth 27   If you don't have something nice to say,
don't say anything at all.   112

Myth 28   It's too late to bring it up now.   117

Myth 29   Love and good sex will make your relationship
affair-proof.   122

Myth 30   Marriage is a fifty-fifty proposition.   126

Myth 31   People don't change.   130

Myth 32   Independence is strength, dependence is weakness.   133

Myth 33   Some people have all the luck.   137

Myth 34   Relationships require a lot of sacrifice.   140

Myth 35   Play is for kids.   144

Myth 36   It's possible to divorce-proof your marriage.   148

Myth 37   Once I attract my ideal mate, my life will be perfect.   150

Myth 38   When it comes to relationships, security is always better. 153

Myth 39   Married couples don't date.   157

Myth 40   Good relationships require more effort
           than they're worth.   161

Afterword   165

Acknowledgments   171

Notes   173

About the Authors   175

Foreword

When I finished reading this book, a wave of gratitude washed over me. I felt somehow freer and a little lighter — as if my load of cultural baggage had just been lightened. Even though I have devoted my life to helping people free themselves from culturally conditioned stereotypes and myths, I still need reminders now and then. I need to be reminded to ask myself, "Where did you get that idea?" when I catch myself automatically accepting commonly held generalizations about life and love. I am grateful to my friends and colleagues Linda and Charlie Bloom for providing such reminders. I think we all need reminders to question our automatic assumptions, and this book does just that.

If you are married or in a traditional intimate relationship, you have probably realized that much of what we consider to be common knowledge about love is simply not true in your particular case. But old beliefs die hard because they reside in the unconscious part of the mind. And marriage comes with its own set of unconscious thought-forms that predispose us to override our true nature and instead conform to expectations we don't even know we hold — like "the passion will fade" or "it's all about compromise."

What if we made it our practice to notice and question every single generalization we've ever learned about how life is and how people are? What if we realized that many of the "givens" in life that we take for granted just might involve a much greater degree of choice and possibility than we are prepared to deal with?

But with more freedom of choice comes more responsibility — *response-ability* to know what you want or value and how hard you're willing to work for it. When we let go of accepted stereotypes — for example, about "what women want" or "what men want" — we must then develop much more refined self-awareness and communication skills to discover what this particular man or woman right here in my bedroom wants. If we opt for an open mind, we then need the skill to discover what this particular here-and-now situation requires of us. This book helps us let go of what we think we know and jump into the unknown of greater possibilities.

My life experience tells me that the Blooms are onto something important here when they remind us, "Especially in relationships, what is true for others may not be true for oneself." They are inviting their readers to throw away the script they were handed by the culture and to discover their own unique way to be in relationship.

Every chapter is a gem — challenging us to look and feel more deeply into the specifics of our particular situation and encouraging us to expand our sense of what is possible. I particularly love the chapter "It's too late to bring it up now" (Myth 28). How often do we invoke this myth as a way of avoiding "making things worse" or "getting back into it"? But with the Blooms' expert guidance, we get a sense that we *can* get back into it — safely, skillfully, and tenderly. As we read their wise words on this and other commonly held myths, we gain clarity that we don't need to rely on outworn beliefs. We can discover things for ourselves! And we see how conscious risk-taking can bring a renewed sense of aliveness to any relationship.

— Susan Campbell, PhD,
coauthor of *Five-Minute Relationship Repair* and author of
Getting Real, Truth in Dating, and *Saying What's Real*

Introduction

True or false:

- Couples with great relationships don't fight.
- Most people expect too much from marriage.
- All the good men/women are already taken.
- Love can heal all wounds.
- If my partner were more like me, we'd have a better relationship.

These are some examples of commonly held beliefs about love, but do these beliefs help or harm your ability to sustain a relationship? Just as importantly, how do you know these beliefs are true? In this book, we call these beliefs "myths" because we consider them to be unsubstantiated ideas that many people accept without question. A myth is defined as "an unproved or false collective belief that is used to justify a social institution." Myths are not personal ideas; they are collective attitudes or stories that possess the power to influence a large number of people. Myths may or may not contain some truth, but whether or not they do, we often repeat them as received wisdom.

Such beliefs can get us into a lot of trouble. When everyone around us seems to share the same ideas, we rarely question them. We don't even see them as beliefs. We regard them as facts, universal truths, or as the way things are, and we act accordingly. When we unquestioningly accept a myth, or a system of thinking and doing things, we become locked into a fixed and rigid perspective that makes it impossible to entertain other points of view. It's the mental equivalent of going through life in a straitjacket.

On the other hand, when we recognize a myth for what it is — a point of view that can be subject to question — we open ourselves to the possibility of considering other ways of seeing and doing things. Relaxing a fixed perspective allows us to access a wider range of responses. This makes it possible for us to be more creative and better able to understand another person's perspective. Suddenly, we can see things from a more expanded point of view, and the world opens up.

Relationships require open-mindedness in order to thrive. Loosening our attachments to widespread myths about love enables the kind of flexibility that strengthens relational bonds. In a relationship, more openness translates into greater mutual understanding.

Our goal in writing this book is to encourage this kind of open and flexible approach to your romantic relationships and committed partnerships. We aren't asking you to stop believing what you believe. We aren't hoping to install a different set of beliefs or a new version of software into your brain. Rather, we want to encourage you to recognize when certain ideas about love have become so deeply embedded in your thinking that it hasn't ever occurred to you to question them. When we step back and see these ideas for what they are — as points of view or opinions, not reality — we free ourselves of inaccurate or unconscious assumptions that may not be serving us, particularly in the context of our relationships.

The ability to consider other perspectives enables us to communicate with greater understanding and trust, which minimizes conflict. Relationships aren't meant to conform to certain standards or fit certain ideals; they aren't right or wrong based on some external measuring stick. Instead, when two people share love, empathy, and compassion, they create a unique partnership that may or may not conform to society's beliefs and definitions.

Freeing ourselves from the hold of rigid beliefs is one of the most empowering things that we can do in our lives and in our relationships. This is an essential part of the process of cultivating the kind of wisdom that characterizes all great relationships. The dictionary defines *wise* as "marked by deep understanding, keen discernment, and a capacity for sound judgment." An essential step in the process of assessing what is true is to evaluate what isn't true. While a myth may contain a kernel of truth, it isn't true in its entirety.

Myths are attractive for several reasons. One is that by adopting them, we feel integrated within a larger community of people who share the same collective perspective. Also, they free us from the responsibility of having to assess people and circumstances on an individual, case-by-case basis. This discernment takes work, and myths provide us with a prepackaged description of "the way things are." But the price that we pay for this "shortcut" is a loss of our ability to see things for ourselves. Another consequence is that living by culturally approved myths blunts our passion for living and diminishes trust in our own judgment.

Accepting myths without questioning them prevents us from experiencing the full measure of freedom, passion, and personal power that is available to us when we take ownership of our own inner authority.

If it is in fact true that the truth will set you free, then perhaps the first step is recognizing when something isn't necessarily true. Believing something to be true when it may not be can be dangerous business indeed. When we act in ways that affirm such untrue beliefs, we can create self-fulfilling prophecies that provide more "evidence" that validates potentially inaccurate views. Over time, we become incapable of seeing these beliefs for what they are, especially since our larger society already holds them as true.

This can be particularly dangerous in relationships, where distinguishing reality from perception can require exceptional powers of discernment. When we act in accordance with beliefs that are unverified, we're not operating from an accurate compass, and so we can end up in places other than where we intended to go.

Another attractive aspect of myths is that they often "feel" true. In relationships, when we experience difficult emotions — such as disappointment, anger, helplessness, guilt, resentment, or some combination of the above — we usually don't attribute those feelings to ungrounded beliefs. Instead, we usually blame our partner or ourselves. It may never occur to us that no one is "at fault." Rather, we may simply need to revise a belief about "the way things are."

Seeing a myth for what it is and questioning its validity

enables us to exert more influence in our relationship. In so doing, we can see our relationship not as a fixed entity but as an evolving process, one that expresses itself moment to moment in a constantly shifting dance. Having cultivated certain ideas and myths over a lifetime, we tend to resist letting them go. To overcome these beliefs, we must develop empathic understanding and respect for our partner, rather than trying to get them to conform to our beliefs. This means being more concerned with listening than with being heard, and with giving rather than getting.

Challenging an assumption requires us first to recognize that what we have held as a fact may not be entirely true. Acknowledging this possibility can be a daunting prospect, since at times it can shake the foundation of our world. No one wants to face that. Yet despite our reluctance to reevaluate the legitimacy of long-standing beliefs, sometimes life experiences trump our resistance to change.

The mind is incredibly powerful, but it's not infallible. It provides wisdom and valuable guidance; it is how we make sense of an overwhelmingly complex world. But if we don't check the accuracy and trustworthiness of the information we receive, our minds can mislead us. If we take shortcuts — by accepting widely held myths and bypassing the process of inquiry — these shortcuts may not lead to reliable pathways to the truth. Especially in relationships, what is true for others may not be true for oneself. Just because many people say something is true doesn't necessarily make it so. Distinguishing belief from reality is itself a process of liberation that frees us to live in accordance with what is true for us.

One indicator of emotional maturity is the number of illusions about the world that one has given up. The process of examining our beliefs can be humbling because it requires us to be willing to detach from previously held positions. Yet the payoff is huge. We gain freedom, passion, creativity, personal power, wisdom, and fulfilling relationships. And all we have to give up are our illusions.

Some things are worth losing. Don't believe everything you think.

Myth 1

And they lived happily ever after.

Who would have ever thought that six harmless words could lead to so much disappointment? How many stories and fairy tales end with this phrase? Each time we hear it, it promises that two lovers — after rising above many hardships and ordeals — have finally merged their hearts as one and will ride off into the sunset together to live forever in the splendor of love's eternal bliss.

Yeah, right.

Many of us may be desperately hoping to be rescued from our insecurities. We long for a relationship that will redeem us, so that we will live (how else?) happily ever after. It can be hard to give up the idea that a relationship will save us from our solitary struggles.

Many of us may also believe that when we enter into a committed partnership, that's the end of the story. Whatever we might be looking for — security, fulfillment, acceptance, unconditional love, support, friendship, intimacy, sex, or any number of other experiences — this valuable thing will be ours forever, we believe, now that we are sharing a life together with this other person. It's no wonder that when the honeymoon ends, as sooner or later it inevitably does, we experience a letdown. Perhaps we even feel real doubt about having chosen the "right" partner.

Most of us believe that marriage will enhance the quality of our lives. Otherwise, why bother? And if it doesn't add what we expect it to, or if it adds something that we don't want it to, we may think one of three things:

1. We're not the "marrying type."
2. We picked the wrong person to marry.
3. Marriage is just a bad idea.

These are understandable thoughts if one believes that marriage is static, a fixed ending, and not a continuation of the story.

But consider the possibility that marriage is not a noun or thing, but a verb, a process. When we get married, we exchange "vows" to act in ways that enhance the quality of each person's life. It's an agreement to take on a set of commitments. The hopes and dreams that we hold for our marriage depend on our willingness to honor the commitments that we have made — not just in our wedding vows, but in our day-to-day agreements as well. A more realistic perspective is to consider marriage as a verb. It is a constantly shifting dynamic process, not a fixed model or concept.

Our ability to cocreate intimacy, trust, and commitment will largely determine what we can accomplish together. This raises the questions: Why do so many marriages end in divorce? Why do so many people live in unhappy marriages? Why don't we see more examples of truly fulfilling relationships?

In part, this is because many people have adopted, at least partially, Western culture's myths about marriage. To most people, "happily ever after" means: If you love each other, you shouldn't fight. A relationship will be consistently blissful forever. You never have to say you're sorry...about anything. You'll never be lonely again, and about a thousand other things that turn out to be untrue. The word for these beliefs is "illusions."

In truth, in any relationship, there will be fights. You will have doubts and moments of uncertainty. You will periodically feel lonely. And when you experience remorse or regrets over something you've done, you will need to apologize. It is in our nature as human beings to have these experiences, whether we are single or partnered, and regardless of who the other person is. It is inherent in the package of being a human being. It's who we are. There isn't any perfect person or perfect relationship. Nobody can fulfill the promise of providing someone else with a permanently blissful life.

Where does this leave us? If we let go of the dream of permanent bliss, and accept the reality of our humanness, we will be less predisposed to experience disappointment, feelings of betrayal, and the grief of disillusionment when our unrealistic expectations are not fulfilled. We are then better able to create a future based upon realistic expectations, ones that are attainable. When we do this, we might enjoy more fully the fruits that truly are available in a committed partnership.

When we see through our illusions, marriage can become the way to experience our heart breaking with sorrow and sometimes cracking open with joy. It is where we can discover how much more of life is available when we become as committed to our partner's well-being as we are to the fulfillment of our own. It is heaven, and it is hell. It is, as Zorba the Greek said, "the full catastrophe."

How much can we open? How many of the illusions that keep our hearts closed can we let go of? How many of our fears can we release in learning to trust another? Can we risk giving up the "security" of our beliefs to gain the experience of our heart's deepest desires? The real question is not "Are we able to see the real challenge of partnership through eyes undistorted by illusion?" Rather: "Are we *willing* to risk being wrong about some of our cherished hopes and beliefs? Are we willing to risk having to challenge, and possibly reassess, what we have held to be true? Are we willing to risk accepting responsibility for the future of our relationship rather than resting in the comfort of our expectations?" When we risk these things, we become a more loving partner rather than a critical judge. It takes lots of patience to do the work of creating deep and lasting trust in a relationship. It also takes time and persistence. We have to be able to persevere, even when we are discouraged and afraid, which from time to time we probably will be.

We don't arrive at an exquisite joining of innermost hearts merely by becoming partners. There is work to do to reap these benefits. Some of those times are not so happy. They contain struggle and ordeals. Going through periods of disappointment and pain is part of the price that we pay for the joys of long-term connection. These difficulties not only provide important lessons, but amplify our appreciation of the joys in our relationship.

If we could experience for one moment what is available to two people who share a pure love, we would gladly undergo any sacrifice that is necessary to achieve it. *The Chinese Book of Changes*, or the *I Ching*, stated over two thousand years ago: "When two people are at one in their inmost hearts, / They shatter even the strength of iron or of bronze. / And when two people understand each other in their inmost hearts, / their words are sweet and strong, like the fragrance of orchids." These words are as true today as they ever were.

Myth 2

People expect too much from relationships.

Charlie: Although it's popular to accuse couples of setting themselves up for disaster by expecting too much from marriage, for many people the problem is exactly the opposite. Many of us don't set our sights high enough. In keeping our expectations low, we may hope to prevent disappointment, but this strategy holds some serious dangers. Limited expectations generate a modest vision of what is possible, and they can easily become self-fulfilling prophecies. The greater the possibilities that we envision, the higher we are likely to set our goals. Where we aim has less to do with what we are actually capable of achieving than with what we believe to be attainable.

Prior to Roger Bannister's breaking of the four-minute mile in 1954, it was deemed impossible for a human being to achieve that feat. Almost immediately after his accomplishment, other runners joined the sub-four-minute-mile club.

Within a decade, several hundred runners had done what ten years previously had been believed impossible. Such is the power of expectations.

When Linda and I got married in 1972, I deliberately set my sights low, all the better to avoid disappointment. I was afraid to hope for anything more than a comfortable arrangement in which we got along reasonably well and didn't fight very much. Talk about low expectations!

Having observed very few examples of thriving long-term relationships, I approached marriage somewhat unenthusiastically. Truth be told, from my perspective, the idea of a happy marriage was an oxymoron. What did appeal to me about marriage was that I saw it as an opportunity to create the kind of family experience that I did not have in my original family. While I hoped to achieve a "corrective experience," I was pessimistic about that happening.

To resolve this contradiction, I developed a strategy of limited engagement. Unfortunately, my strategy not only failed to prevent disappointment, but it left me frequently feeling resentful and frustrated. What I hadn't factored into the equation was the fact that my head wasn't the only part of me that was engaged. As French philosopher Blaise Pascal famously said, "The heart has its reasons of which reason knows nothing," and my heart had its own agenda. Ultimately, it insisted on having its say.

In my case, the inevitable breakdown took the form of complaints that both Linda and I directed at each other with increasing frequency and intensity until things got to the breaking point. I minimized the amount of time that we spent together and maximized the amount of time that I spent on other "more important" things, namely work. In so doing, I reasoned that there would be minimal danger of conflict, and we could maintain an adequate degree of connection. Translation: Just enough connection to prevent a divorce. Unfortunately, while this was my preferred method, it didn't work for Linda. And she made it a point to let me know. Repeatedly.

Since my idea of minimalism flew directly in the face of Linda's desire for wholehearted intimacy as well as my own denied desire for the same thing, I had a conflict not only with her but within myself. In trying to settle for what was inherently an unsatisfying relationship, I was both living a lie and trying to force this same thing on Linda, who fortunately was unwilling to compromise her dream of a deeply loving marriage, regardless of the emotional risks that this entailed. The truth was that I was afraid that I was unfit for a truly fulfilling relationship and that it made no sense to even try for it. I believed that to hope for more would be naïve and unrealistic, since it seemed that no one has that kind of marriage anyway, except in the movies. These beliefs were all basically rationalizations to avoid the risk of genuine emotional intimacy.

When Linda and I finally did reach the brink of divorce, my desire to maintain our connection overrode my commitment to avoiding disappointment. That was when things began to change. This transition, which occurred over twenty-five years ago, has been ongoing and has transformed our relationship in ways that have had lasting effects on us both.

It was only because Linda refused to settle for the kind of mediocrity that I was willing to accept that I finally chose to jump in with both feet. Had she been unwilling to put our marriage on the line as she did, there is no question in my mind that we would not be together today.

Without Linda's vision of what was possible for us, and

her insistence that we owe it to ourselves and each other to go for the gold, rather than the tin medal, I would never have chosen to join her in her vision.

I learned from Linda that marriage takes more than time and effort. It takes vision, courage, commitment, determination, and patience, lots of patience. I didn't have much of these when I opted out of my game and into hers. But with Linda's help and support, I came to join her in what became *our* vision.

What we have come to enjoy together is infinitely more than I had believed possible for us, and it has exceeded Linda's hopes as well.

These days, I'm not so afraid of being disappointed. I've grown to appreciate disappointments and to trust that I no longer really need the protection of minimal hopes. Linda and I take turns challenging ourselves to find out what's truly possible as we work together. It's not only for us, but also for the many people whom we touch and are touched by.

We have found that while the mind seeks a comfortable and easy relationship, the heart has other concerns. The heart could care less about risk management, control, safety, and security. Its desires have to do with passion, connection, truthfulness, intimacy, aliveness, and joyfulness — experiences that exist outside of the bounds of pragmatic considerations. The desires of the heart need to be met and included in the equation. To the degree they are not, we will be unfulfilled, regardless of how much security, status, or economic success we achieve. As the saying goes, "You can't ever get enough of what you really don't need."

In the words of Bob Dylan, "He who isn't busy being born is busy dying." This applies not only to individuals but to marriages as well. The notion that we can put things on cruise control and sail through life together with a minimum of engagement and still experience a high quality of life exists in the domain of fantasy, not reality. To be busy being born requires the willingness to show up, to risk, to tell the truth to others and to ourselves about what we truly desire, what we fear, what we long for, and what brings passion into our lives. Marriage, to quote Stephen Levine, is "the ultimate danger sport." It is not for the faint of heart. It is the path that tends to provoke the most resistance, since we tend to attract and marry people who are our counterparts.

With Linda's help, I have discovered that this path can also be the path of greatest fulfillment, of greatest joy, and of greatest possibility. It is the path that insists not only that we awaken to our deepest desires but that we engage others in that same challenge: the pursuit of the fulfillment of what truly matters to us and the fulfillment of who we are as human beings. Having low expectations can become a self-fulfilling prophecy. When we raise our expectations and link them to a powerful intention and a clear commitment, and we create a strong alliance with our partner, it becomes possible not only to override our fears and concerns but to achieve greatness together beyond anything we had previously imagined.

Myth 3

If we fight, it means
we're not meant for each other.

When does the honeymoon end? Is it the first time you realize that your mate isn't all you had hoped for? Or maybe it is when you discover that sometimes their cheerful optimism can turn to resentment or depression for no apparent reason. Do you remember your first fight? Have you ever wondered whether you made a mistake in your selection of a partner? Do you experience anger, frustration, hostility, or resentment toward your partner, perhaps more times than you care to admit? Many people can take these feelings as an indication that something is seriously out of line in their marriage or relationship. If you're human, you've also probably attempted to influence your partner's feelings, attitudes, or behaviors, only to discover that this just creates a new problem.

Most of us spend between twelve and twenty years of our lives in school, yet nowhere are we really taught how to sustain and enhance the quality of our relationships. We hope and pray that despite our ignorance we can make it work anyway. And when the inevitable conflicts arise, we may find ourselves entrenched or embattled with our partner.

Though conflict may not be avoidable in marriage, it is not necessarily a foreshadowing of doom. Differences in opinions, feelings, temperaments, and even values are an inherent aspect of relationships. In fact, we generally select partners who will help us to expand our inner and outer lives by offering a broader range of perspectives. Nevertheless, opening up to these opportunities for growth can at times be excruciatingly uncomfortable. Often it is easier to tell ourselves that our relationship is "just not meant to be." And yet how many of us know couples who called it quits in frustration, only to turn around and play out the same pattern with another person?

What if the object of relationships is not to eliminate conflict but to work with it in an effective, responsible, and conscious way? What if each breakdown that occurs between two people holds the seeds of each becoming a more loving and wise person? What if your experience of your relationship has more to do with you than it does with your partner? What if, despite your doubts, you haven't made a mistake or wrong choice in the selection of a mate, and you really do have the perfect partner for the lessons that you're in this relationship to learn?

Asking these questions begins the process of inquiry that takes us beyond the models, expectations, and beliefs we all have about relationships. In this way we discover and create new possibilities. One of the biggest barriers in the development of a great partnership is one's own set of preconceived beliefs about conflict and anger.

Observing the suffering of other couples who struggle in

their marriages, it's easy to presume that marriages inevitably break down sooner or later and that, for many couples, the breakdown is permanent. It's easy to wonder, "Who's next? Is it us?" Yet the tendency to feel resignation and hopelessness in the face of fear is a choice, and we often make it out of a desire to avoid looking more directly at some difficult questions. Here are some of those questions:

- How might I have contributed to the current situation?
- What beliefs about myself or others might I be validating by holding on to my position?
- What am I so attached to being right about, and why?
- What, if anything, might I have done that I need to reveal to my partner?
- What fear is underneath my fear of losing (or staying in) this relationship?
- What unfulfilled needs or desires have I failed to disclose to my partner, and why?
- What forms of manipulation have I used to try to coerce my partner into accommodating my desires?
- Am I making my partner responsible for fulfilling needs within myself that are my responsibility and not theirs?

The focus of these questions is to understand the part we play in a conflict. They require us to redirect the focus of our attention away from our partner and to look instead at ourselves, at our role in the chain of events that has led to a breakdown or fight. Doing so does not absolve one's partner of their responsibility for the conflict, but it empowers us to focus our energies on the only person that we have the power to control in this scenario, and that is ourselves.

Focusing on our own responsibility can make us feel vulnerable, but this can help our partner to feel less defensive and, consequently, more inclined to listen to our concerns and needs. Such openness promotes a more conciliatory and cooperative attitude between both partners, thus interrupting the cycle of defensiveness that turns ordinary differences into destructive conflict.

There is no guarantee that our partner will reciprocate if we lower our own defenses. Our vulnerability is merely an invitation to respond with vulnerability. However, without this invitation, our partner might feel they have no choice but to remain defended. When we model vulnerability, we give them a chance to show whether they too are willing to disarm themselves of their own defenses.

By interrupting our defensive patterns, we can move beyond the concerns of day-to-day survival and raise new questions about the greater possibilities of our relationship, such as, "How great could our relationship really be?" Once we understand that much more is possible than we may have previously believed, old dreams are reawakened and new ones come into being along with a newfound confidence in our ability to realize them.

Paradoxically, it is only when we accept that there is no magic involved in the process of relationship-building, and no perfect person with whom we can effortlessly cocreate the partnership of our dreams, that we begin to experience the degree of ease and joy we hope for. But first we need to free ourselves of our limiting beliefs and expectations. To find the partner of your dreams, it's necessary to first *become* the partner of your dreams. In so doing, you become irresistible to the person that you have been waiting for, whether you haven't met that person yet or you've been married to him or her for thirty years!

Myth 4

A happy childhood is a prerequisite to a great relationship.

I f this myth were true, most of us would be doomed to relationship hell. Fortunately, it's not, and we're not. It turns out that it is possible even for people who have lived in difficult, abusive, or horrible circumstances to create loving and healthy relationships. Many of the couples we know who are living deeply fulfilling lives grew up in situations that were far from ideal, and some were downright wretched. We also know people who grew up in families in which there was an abundance of happiness, love, and security who have terrible track records regarding their relationships. Naturally, growing up in a happy family is what we want, but it is not an essential factor in creating successful relationships as an adult. So, you might ask, what then are the critical factors that determine the likelihood of relationship success?

While there is no way to accurately assess the percentage of people who came from unhealthy families, it's reasonably safe to state that many people feel they didn't get the great start in life they wanted. Perhaps they grew up under less-than-ideal circumstances that included various forms of addiction, abuse, or neglect. While such circumstances pose significant obstacles that can impede physical, emotional, and intellectual development, they are by no means insurmountable given the right kind of support, resources, and motivation in adulthood. Overcoming such hardships isn't easy, but it's simply untrue that anyone who has grown up in a dysfunctional family cannot hope to create a healthy adult relationship.

Those who grew up in neglectful or abusive families do often share a common obstacle, which is an internalized belief that they are not worthy of being treated with respect or love. In some families, children may not have felt wanted or valued, things may have seemed chaotic or unpredictable, and children may have felt insecure much of the time. They may have felt in the way, ignored, or overly controlled. Children can't change their circumstances, and this can leave them feeling powerless and unlovable. Children tend to take things personally and assume that they are deserving of whatever treatment they receive, good or bad. This adds an extra burden to anyone who has had to deal with childhood adversity. Added difficulties are always challenging, but there is a difference between what is difficult and what is impossible.

Those who were fortunate enough as children to have positive esteem mirrored back to them from loving adults are more likely to come into adulthood feeling more secure in themselves and safe in the world. They often internalize the belief that they are valued, wanted, cherished, honored, and loved. Still, high self-esteem is no guarantee of a successful

relationship, just as low self-esteem is no guarantee of an un-
successful relationship.

The factors that seem most relevant to the creation of successful adult relationships have more to do with our capacity
to learn, to become more emotionally mature, and to detach
from unhealthy behavioral patterns, as well as a commitment
to heal the places in our inner lives that are in need of acceptance and forgiveness. Everyone possesses a "shadow" side,
those qualities that we deem to be unacceptable and shameful.
Working to integrate and come to terms with our shadow is
one of the most significant things that we can do to enhance
our ability to create successful relationships.

When it comes to our childhoods, most people fall some-
where between the extremes of the abysmal and the ideal. We
may feel a mix of worth and worthlessness, unlovability and
lovability. Many choose psychotherapy to help treat problems
of low self-esteem, anxiety, depression, or addictive patterns,
but there are other means available through which we can heal
past wounds. One of them is creating a committed partnership.
Committed partnerships provide us with the means through
which we can expose the unhealed parts of ourselves to someone who has the capacity and desire to accept those aspects of
us that we deem to be unacceptable. A committed partnership
is not necessarily a substitute for therapy, but it can provide us
with the kind of experience that affects our sense of value as a
person.

Being treated with acceptance and respect can heal the
places in ourselves that have been wounded and help to re-
store a sense of wholeness. As we come more fully into integrity, our capacity to give and receive love increases and

deepens. Loving partnerships tend to diminish anxiety and promote a sense of security. These relationships, due to their very nature, expose whatever within us has been intentionally or unconsciously concealed, thus providing us with opportunities to bring compassion to ourselves and, by extension, to others.

Marriage isn't inherently healing. We don't automatically experience happiness when we engage in a committed partnership. The shared decision to use the relationship as a means of promoting mutual well-being for both partners is the primary factor that determines whether we create a great or a not-so-great partnership. Not only is it possible to have a great relationship even after growing up in difficult circumstances, but the pain of our past experience can actually become the motivation that drives our commitment to do the necessary work to create the kind of fulfillment that we were denied as a child.

The past does not have to dictate the future. It is only one factor, and not necessarily the most significant one, that influences future possibilities. We can recover, heal, and grow beyond the limitations of our past experiences, but only if we trust that this is possible. The person who believes that something is possible and the person who believes that something is not possible are both correct. There is great power in our beliefs, and they can easily become self-fulfilling prophecies. If we are convinced that we are handicapped by our past, then we will act in accordance with that belief and ultimately prove ourselves right. On the other hand, if we refuse to accept the notion that our future is determined by our past, we can do the work to recover from our wounds. In doing so, not only will we free ourselves from the limits of old beliefs, but we will be on our way to creating the life we have always hoped for. We can come from serious dysfunction, addiction, abuse, or neglect and still create a golden relationship. It's not about the past; it's about our belief in our ability to fulfill our vision for the future. And it's about commitment.

Myth 5

Marriages inevitably get flat, stale, and boring over time.

Yes, becoming bored with one's spouse can be a real problem. It's a frequently voiced complaint that therapists often hear from their clients. Fortunately, this condition can usually be easily fixed. Unfortunately, the source of the problem is generally in the last place that clients want to look: that would be themselves.

Sometimes the very things that originally attracted us to our partner — perhaps those wonderful qualities of predictability, stability, and dependability they bring into our fragmented and tumultuous life — can in time become the source of our greatest irritation. What at one point in a relationship feels like security, at another feels oppressively boring. Your partner probably hasn't changed, and neither have you. Those qualities in them that you initially found so attractive are still there; it's just that they are less evident because you are focusing on those aspects of the relationship that you find dissatisfying.

There will always be things about your partner that displease you. If you're like most people, you may have a belief that if you were with someone else — someone more interesting, exciting, imaginative, passionate, creative, and so on — you would be happier. Not likely. If you had really wanted other qualities than what made your partner so attractive at first, you would have set your sights on that different kind of a person. You didn't, and it's likely that you didn't make a mistake in your choice of a partner. Like most of us, you chose the kind of person that would fulfill certain needs in your life. Some needs you were conscious of, some perhaps not, and yet no one person (except our fantasy lover) can fulfill all our needs.

The good news is that you have the ability to change the quality of your experience with your partner even if your partner never changes. The solution is two-fold: Stop dwelling on what you don't like, and start focusing on what it is that you love and appreciate. Focus on those qualities that you initially found attractive and that make your life more comfortable than it would have been without this person. Don't keep your appreciation to yourself; share it. Don't let a day pass without expressing your gratitude. Don't be surprised if your words of acknowledgment don't change your partner.

If we can't change a situation, then our challenge is to change the way we think about and respond to it. Sometimes boredom can result from repressed anger and resentment that hasn't been acknowledged and expressed. When we move from the disempowered position of wishing and hoping that the other person would change, and instead take responsibility for how we deal with the reality in front of us, we can look inside to see if there are some truths that are waiting to be spoken that could bring more vitality into a flat relationship.

Boredom can also be a manifestation of not paying sufficiently close attention. Check to see if you took a snapshot of your partner years ago and put it in your mental photo album. Are you still gazing at the same old page? We can look through fresher eyes to see how our partner may have changed. Then, we can acknowledge those changes to ourselves and also speak words of appreciation and gratitude to our partner, recognizing their growth and development.

Last, but certainly not least: People who are bored are often bored with their own lives. Are there unfulfilled dreams that you haven't tried to realize? Are you making excuses for what you don't have in your life rather than going after what you want? What actions have you been unwilling to take that could possibly lead to a higher level of excitement or passion in your life? Quit boring yourself with your complaints, and get out there and start taking some risks. Get clear about the things that you want to accomplish, and start doing them, rather than complaining about your partner or making excuses as to why you can't do what you really want to do.

It's possible that if you do some or all of these things, your relationship and your life in general will become more interesting, even exhilarating! It might also become more challenging and stimulating. Who knows? You might enjoy living on the edge. And when your partner sees how much fun you're having, he or she might even decide to join you!

Myth 6

Once a cheater, always a cheater.

Few people would argue with the idea that honesty is the best policy. Policies, however, are not always adhered to. Regardless of how much we may desire to live a life of integrity, in which we "walk the talk" and live in accordance with our inner principles, it's likely that there will be times that we miss the mark. Nobody's perfect. Every relationship needs to have some room for slippage.

Great relationships require a high level of integrity. When a violation of trust, large or small, occurs, it's important to examine the conditions that contributed to the situation, as well as to engage in a healing process that will restore trust and goodwill.

Cheating refers to sexual misconduct, which is a form of betrayal. A betrayal is a broken agreement, implicit or explicit, that is considered vital to maintain a trusting relationship. The capacity of a relationship to recover from a betrayal has a lot to do with each person's response, particularly that of the person seen as the transgressor. The more open and nondefensive that person is, the more likely it is that there will be resolution. When both partners are committed to resolution as an outcome, the likelihood increases exponentially. The lies and denials that are used to cover up a transgression can do much more damage than the violation itself. Even if the lie is never uncovered and the offense is not revealed, there can still be great harm done to the foundation of the relationship. Trust is inevitably damaged even when secrets go undetected. Most but not all betrayals and acts of deceit can be healed. While there is no generic template to apply to these situations, here are some guidelines that can facilitate the recovery process.

Acknowledge your actions: If you have betrayed your partner, tell your partner before, not after, they find out for themselves. The sooner the better. The longer you have been living a lie, the deeper the damage, the lesser the likelihood of a full recovery, and the longer the healing process takes. Acknowledging your transgression before your partner affirms it from another source creates a higher level of trust than waiting until you've been found out.

Get honest: After admitting your actions, commit yourself to zero tolerance for dishonesty in your relationship from now on. Even after you've successfully demonstrated your commitment, don't be surprised if your partner needs a lot of evidence that you are trustworthy before they'll be ready to take your word at face value. Rebuilding trust takes time and will require patience on your part.

Address every question: To build trust after a betrayal, don't be defensive in response to your partner's need for information. They need to make sure that you aren't withholding anything else, and they probably have a lot of questions that only you can answer. Be guided by the question, "Is this information necessary for the healing of our relationship?" Keep in mind that your intention in this process is to communicate in a way that will restore goodwill. Try to see the questions as an opportunity for you to demonstrate the kind of truth-telling that your partner needs in order to begin to trust you again. Even if the questions seem repetitive or unnecessary, your partner may need to hear certain information in multiple ways in order to come to terms with the situation.

Listen to your partner's feelings: Both partners need to listen to what the other expresses. Don't analyze, evaluate, judge, or reason with your partner about what they feel. Listening without disputing is not equivalent to agreeing with someone's point of view. It's possible to listen respectfully even if you don't see eye-to-eye about everything. Feelings aren't necessarily rational, but they are real. Each person not only needs a chance to express what they want to say, but also needs to feel that what they've said has been heard and received by the other.

Be patient: If you are at fault, reassure your partner that they can take as much time as they need to rebuild trust. The process may take longer than you think it should, and this will require self-restraint and patience on your part. In the end, it is likely to bring about a deepening of the connection between the two of you. Resist the temptation to urge your partner to "get over it." Instead, reassure them, saying something like: "I know that I am serious about this commitment, and I understand that you need more time to see the evidence and to trust me again. I can give you all the time you need."

Take responsibility for your actions: Acknowledge the truth of what you've done, and particularly at first, avoid any explanations, rationalizations, excuses, or justifications for your behavior. In time, you both might be able to view things from a larger context, and identify the conditions in the relationship that may have contributed to the situation, but that will come later.

Stay focused on your intention to heal the damage: When both partners remain committed to repairing the relationship, the likelihood of a favorable outcome is greatly increased.

Most of the time, recovery is a real possibility. The benefits of reconciliation greatly outweigh the costs. Take it from the couples who have found out for themselves. It takes honesty and self-reflection on the part of both partners. Affairs can be extremely damaging to relationships, but they need not be fatal. Many couples have told us that, in the end, the crisis that came from the betrayal ultimately led to a profound deepening of the love and trust that the partners currently share.

When both partners are willing to become not only more honest but responsible for creating and maintaining a high level of integrity in the relationship, the likelihood of going outside the marriage is greatly reduced. If you expect your partner to violate your fidelity vows again, you run the risk of having that expectation become a self-fulfilling prophecy. It takes courage to resist the temptation to give up this expectation in favor of committing to repair broken trust and to create a more fulfilling partnership. Of course, there is no guarantee, but many people who have taken this risk have found it to be well worth the effort. If you are facing this choice, there is only one way to find out. The work of recovery from a violation of trust in a committed partnership takes time and effort and can be humbling. The stakes are high, but the benefits of doing the work are enormous. A successful healing can transform a damaged partnership into a sacred union.

Myth 7

All you need is love.

The Beatles were on the money with almost all their songs, but on this one, I'm afraid that they got it wrong. Beatles fans who embraced this song as the holy truth probably found themselves deeply disappointed. Love is not, in fact, all you need. And despite the Beatles' reassurance that "It's eeeeasy," that also isn't the case. Many die-hard Beatles fans still cling to this song's promise, but in our experience, it's just not true.

Of course, some things and some people *are* easy to love, like a newborn baby, especially if it's your own, or a cute little puppy, or Mom's delicious homemade chocolate chip cookies, or that beautiful Porsche convertible that just pulled up next to you at the stoplight. But to deeply love another adult human being, seeing their every aspect as being divine and perfect, with complete vulnerability and openheartedness....

As you may have noticed, realizing that isn't all that eeeeasy. It is easy to have loving feelings toward someone when we find

29

them physically attractive, fun to be with, funny, charming,
and sweet smelling, and especially if they laugh at our jokes!
But being strongly attracted to another person isn't necessarily love. It is easy, though, to confuse the two. Love asks more
of us than simply feeling a strong desire for another person.
It demands that we put our own preferences aside from time
to time and replace them with a desire to serve our partner. It
requires that we must:

- be willing to be wrong.
- resist the temptation to project blame on our beloved when we feel disappointed or upset.
- experience more lessons in humility than most of
  us want to.
- restrain ourselves when we feel the impulse to say
  or do something that would gratify our ego at the
  expense of our partner's happiness.
- constantly seek to discover what we can give to
  our partner, rather than living in the question
  "What's in it for me?"
- be vulnerable rather than defensive when we feel
  threatened.

And this is just for starters. Inherent in the myth that "love
is all you need" is the notion that love is enough to:

- get you through the hard times that tend to show
  up for all of us.
- avoid conflict.
- overcome all obstacles.
- heal all wounds.
- prevent future wounding.
- keep you healthy.

- never be lonely again.
- live happily ever after.
- make you whole when you feel broken.

Not that love won't make navigating the road through life's inevitable difficulties a lot less painful. It will enhance your life with feelings of goodwill, happiness, and well-being. It might even enhance your health and extend your longevity. So please, go ahead, and as another sixties song advised, "Put a little love in your heart." But don't get too attached to the idea that love is all you need, lest you find yourself deeply disappointed when that does not turn out to be the case. This can lead to unnecessary doubt. If you love your beloved, and things aren't going according to the way they "should," you might decide he or she doesn't love you.

All of which begs the question: "What else is it that you need in addition to love?" Funny you should ask. Besides love, here are a few other things that will help get you through the night:

- Skill in dealing with the differences that show up in *all* relationships, even the ones with lots of love.
- Patience for those not-so-rare occasions when things don't go exactly the way you had planned.
- The ability to really listen and to resist the temptation to interrupt or "correct" your partner when you disagree.
- Acceptance of your own mistakes. Otherwise, you will judge and reject in your partner whatever you judge and reject in yourself.
- Compassion for both your partner and you-know-who.
- The integrity to walk your talk.

- The courage to keep trying.
- The vision to see what you stand to experience when your intentions are aligned with your partner's.
- Trust and trustworthiness.
- And last but definitely not least, a good sense of humor. You're going to need it.

Myth 8

When you've lost that loving feeling, it's gone, gone, gone.

Jeremy and Ellen had been together for a while when he told her that he loved her but that he was not *in* love with her. When Ellen asked Jeremy what he meant, he couldn't really explain it. Ellen said that it was "something about no longer feeling the same way that he used to, but nothing more specific." She said that she knew where this was going, and sure enough, she was right. "The next thing he said was, 'I want us to be friends, good friends.' Well, the very *last* thing I wanted was to be his friend. I don't ever want to see him again!"

Ellen was upset, to put it mildly. Actually, she was outraged, hurt, confused, and brokenhearted. If you've ever been in Ellen's shoes, you probably know how she felt. And if you've ever been in Jeremy's shoes, you probably know what he felt, and perhaps you had just as much difficulty articulating it.

"I love you, but I'm not *in* love with you." We have heard so many people describe how they either sent or received this message that we decided to explore what it might really mean. Here are some of the things people have told us this statement meant to them:

- I'm not enjoying our relationship anymore, and I don't really want to continue being in it.
- I don't think that we're a good fit.
- The thrill and intensity of the initial romance has faded, and now it's not as much fun as it used to be.
- I think you're a nice person, but I'm holding out for someone better who will be easy, fun, and hot to be with all the time.
- I'm beginning to notice that we have "issues," and I don't like where this is going.
- I want to get out before it gets too difficult to leave.
- I'm thinking that you have longer-range plans for us than I do.
- I'm feeling claustrophobic in our relationship, and I don't know how to talk about it without making you upset.
- I'm having feelings that are uncomfortable and disturbing, and I think that you're causing them.
- I don't want to hurt or anger you because then you might do the same to me, so I'll try to say what I need to in a way that won't upset you.
- You don't make me feel the way you used to.
- I want to slow down or cool off our relationship.
- I want out.

Not every relationship is meant to last forever. Partners aren't always in agreement with each other in regard to whether it's time to call it quits. But how do you know if it's really over or if the discomfort that you feel indicates that there's work to do before you can upgrade your relationship to the next level? Knowing the difference between these two is crucial for anyone who seeks to deepen the quality of their connection. Like the song goes, "You gotta know when to hold 'em, and know when to fold 'em." The impulse to fold can be strong when things get difficult. There is often a tendency to justify our decision by telling ourselves that it's just not working anymore, rather than looking at some of the deeper causes for feelings of boredom, resentment, or discontent. The problem with leaving too soon is that you may miss the very thing that you originally signed up for in the first place.

That "loving feeling" is often another term for infatuation, which literally means to be in a state of unreasonable and short-lived passion. The word *fatuous* means deluded and self-deceiving. Infatuation is nature's way of getting us together so that we can perpetuate the species. When we are in a state of infatuation, we are quite literally "out of our minds," and our brains are drenched in hormones and chemicals like endorphins and oxytocin that produce irresistible sensations, feelings, and urges. Fortunately, the experience of infatuation is temporary. "Temporary," however, can range from minutes to years. The question then has to do with how we deal with the inevitable letdown when that loving feeling is lost. One way is to look for someone else with whom we can re-create this experience. Some people are so in love with the feeling of falling in love that they become serial lovers, sometimes in the hopes of finding that person with whom there will be no fading effect. Some just decide that they are not the settling-down type. Then there are some who know that infatuation is impermanent and that something even better awaits those who are willing to investigate the deeper reaches of relationship: that which lies beyond sensory pleasure.

Unfortunately, there is no universal answer to the question, "How do you know when to hang in there and when to cut your losses?" It is a pretty safe bet that if you don't feel that you've given things your very best shot, then it's worth hanging in there a bit longer and making the extra effort. Sometimes we think that we're out of gas, but there's actually more in the reserve tank. Athletes experience what they refer to as a "second wind," which often occurs after the point at which they feel completely depleted.

Being in relationship, as many of us know from our own experience, is not unlike being an endurance athlete or a marathon runner. It may require the willingness to hang in there and go past the point where you feel like quitting in order to find the strength needed to finish the race. The saying "You can't find out how far you can go unless you're willing to risk going too far" definitely applies here. The fear of hanging in there too long is often driven by the concern that, in doing so, we may risk getting hurt or reactivating previous, incompletely healed wounds. Willingly exposing ourselves to that risk helps us cultivate the kind of resilience that enables us to expand our capacity to endure and overcome obstacles that may show up on the path.

There can, however, come a time when it may be necessary to call it quits. When you've given your best, when you've kept your focus on doing your own work instead of focusing on how your partner is doing, when you've learned the lessons that your relationship has provided you, and when continuing to make the effort leaves you feeling diminished and depleted rather than inspired, it could be time to consider the alternative. To do so at this point is not a matter of giving up; rather, it's letting go of the hopes that you had of the relationship, allowing yourself to celebrate the rich experiences you shared, and grieving the loss.

Feelings come and go, and desire and attraction are two feelings that we may or may not experience toward our partner at any given time. When feelings of attraction or desire diminish or disappear, it's generally better to acknowledge it to ourselves and our partner out of an intention to identify and, if possible, correct a negative condition in the relationship. The sooner we recognize the source of our feelings of discontent, the sooner we can address them and minimize damage and suffering.

Not all relationships can be restored or preserved when the flame cools, but the sooner this circumstance is recognized, the greater the likelihood it will be. Both partners are more likely to still be motivated to find out whether the partnership is salvageable. Delaying things is likely to make an eventual breakup more, not less, likely.

Sometimes it looks as if the fire is out and only smoldering ashes remain. It only takes an ember to reignite the fire. All too many couples have given up hope when, in fact, the possibility of regaining passion is still alive. If we engage with others consciously and responsibly, then each relationship provides us with greater insights that contribute to wisdom and love. Regardless of the outcome of that relationship, we bring these insights to all our relationships, current as well as future. The gifts on this path are abundant and invaluable. They include courage, commitment, imagination, compassion, and, oh yes, patience — and lots of it — because it doesn't happen overnight. And you get to benefit from these gifts no matter what happens. Overall, that sounds like a pretty good deal.

Myth 9

All differences need to be reconciled.

Before Leah married Jason, she thought that their differences would naturally diminish as they got to know each other better. She discovered that their different points of view and behaviors not only didn't go away but actually became inflamed, to the point where it looked as if they might have to end their marriage. Things looked hopeless to both of them. They were caught up in a downward spiral in which they were each trying to convert the other to their own way of seeing things. Their efforts were destroying the love and goodwill they shared.

They fought about all kinds of things, like how early to leave for the airport, whether to have a cat or a dog, whether to stay in or go out with friends; anything could set them off. The concerns that they were arguing over weren't the real issues. It was really the sensitivity that both of them had about feeling controlled.

Whenever Jason took a stand about something, Leah responded defensively. She hated it when he disagreed with her. She thought that if he loved her, he wouldn't argue with her. Whenever she felt this way, her fear caused her to amp up her efforts to control him, and they continually found themselves locked into painful power struggles. They were living like enemies, hadn't had sex for months, and things were getting worse.

When Leah brought up the possibility of getting professional help, they got into a power struggle about that, too, because Jason's philosophy was that if you put your mind to something, and work hard to straighten out your problems, you should be able to take care of things on your own. After going around and around for weeks, Jason grudgingly agreed to accompany Leah to see a counselor. Once in the counseling office, they both participated actively in the sessions, and things soon began to turn a corner.

Jason and Leah shared the same fear: they believed that if they didn't eliminate their differences and homogenize as a couple, their marriage would self-destruct. One of the most important things that they learned was that it wasn't their differences that were the problem, but their efforts to convert each other to their respective points of view. As they each began to trust that they could be different, and that their differences would not and need not go away, they both relaxed their need to get the other to change.

Changing old habits isn't easy and can take time. Fortunately, most couples have plenty of "learning opportunities" to become more appreciative of their differences and more accepting of their respective ways of being in the world. Even lifelong "hotheads" can develop greater tolerance, acceptance, patience, and forgiveness, once they become more skilled in the art of nonreactive listening. It's not about homogenizing as a couple but about becoming more uniquely yourself. For most couples, their individual differences are often what initially drew them to each other. These differences provide the chemistry that great relationships thrive on.

It's our differences, not our similarities, that deepen and expand our relationship and our world. If the absence of irreconcilable differences were a requirement for staying married, there would be very few married couples today. Even the most successful marriages contain them. Of course, some differences can be deal breakers: things one or both partners can't tolerate. But in our experience, when there is a foundation of love and respect, this situation is less likely to occur. Only a small portion of the differences that most couples start out with are actually reconcilable. Differences are not the problem. It's our conflicts over difference that lead to trouble.

Leah and Jason salvaged a marriage that was on life support by being willing to stop playing out lifelong patterns of control and manipulation. They were willing to risk it all to go for the real gold that is available in committed partnerships. In taking the risk of letting go of control, they discovered not only that their worst fears did not materialize, but that they each felt safer and more connected to the other. Detaching from the illusion of control produced a very different result than either of them believed it would. Sometimes being wrong isn't such a bad thing.

Myth 10

Time heals all wounds.

While the saying "Time heals all wounds" can provide comfort when we are suffering, there is a point at which this attitude can become the source of greater misery. It's true that pain and suffering can diminish over time, but waiting for suffering to lift, tolerating pain with the expectation that time alone will make things better, can extend and even exacerbate our suffering. What may be called for is a more proactive stance in our recovery process. Accepting the reality of our experience is unquestionably an important aspect of healing and growth, but when this stance is motivated by a desire to avoid responsible action, it can amplify rather than diminish our unhappiness. When we simply wait for time to heal our wounds rather than viewing ourselves as a responsible agent in the process, we may be trying to rationalize a passive (safer) response to our circumstances. Recovery requires more than patience and acceptance. We also must be willing to take effective action. Otherwise, we risk getting stuck in a destructive holding pattern. It's a matter not of choosing between acceptance and proactivity, but rather of embodying them both.

When we are wounded, physically or emotionally, we are called upon to exercise both patience, in order to allow the natural healing process to occur, as well as intentionality and responsibility, in order to support that process by doing our part. There are always things that we can do besides letting nature run its course, particularly in the matter of relationships. Sometimes crises can challenge us to make necessary life changes. Making such changes is not easy and can feel dangerous. We tend to want to hold on to what we know rather than risk stepping into the unknown. Taking this risk requires being willing to become the change we wish to see in our relationship and to accept the fact that "if it's to be, it's up to me." This doesn't guarantee that things will get better; it just makes it more likely that they will. In assuming this responsibility, we become clearer about what we want and need in order to thrive. As our vision becomes clearer, we become aware of options that were not previously apparent to us.

People cite many reasons for staying in troubled relationships without making much effort to change things. Some stay on behalf of children, for financial reasons, out of fear of being alone, or to avoid the disapproval of family or friends, to name a few examples. Many hope that things will somehow improve in time, yet this waiting can cause us to feel trapped, victimized, helpless, ineffectual, or resentful. Breaking out of this mind-set requires becoming proactive and asking ourselves what we want to happen or change in the relationship.

It's not a matter of denying our grievances or whatever disturbs us. Rather, we direct our attention to what we can do that might move things in the right direction. Making this shift in our perspective can interrupt old patterns that may have contributed to our present impasse. This process requires us to identify what we need to do to strengthen ourselves in order to become a more capable life partner. It also means releasing the belief that the other person needs to change before what we desire can come about. By choosing to be passive or reactive rather than proactive, we reaffirm our sense of powerlessness.

When we redirect our attention from our partner's shortcomings to what we can do to bring about our desired outcome, not only do our actions change but our mood often shifts from resentment and resignation to hopefulness and possibility. This improves our chances of success, even if it does not guarantee it, and it makes the process more rewarding for both partners.

By becoming proactive, one of two things will happen. Either your partner will respond positively to your efforts, or they won't. Genuine change generally occurs gradually over time, so it's best not to expect instant transformation. If your partner doesn't come around immediately, don't quit trying; keep doing what you know you need to do. At some point, probably within weeks or months, rather than days, the answer to the "should I stay or should I go" question will in all likelihood become apparent, but only if you keep your focus on yourself and continue doing your own work.

Reaching this point of clarity requires an all-out effort. One way or the other, we no longer wait and hope for change. We leave the holding pattern where there is no movement. Either way, our mood, self-esteem, and energy level go up.

This process requires us to be willing to risk losing the relationship. At times, when a relationship is not working, it has to die in its old form. The fear of letting go can be frightening and cause us to hold on to dysfunctional patterns. Yet sometimes we have to risk loss in order to move from breakdown to breakthrough rather than breakup.

When both partners are each doing their own work, the chances for a breakthrough are greatly increased. There is no guarantee that you will come through this process with an intact partnership. Some couples are just mismatched. The most gifted therapist and the most hardworking couple cannot be certain of what the end result will be.

Even when the outcome is separation, the process may be considered successful if the quality of the relationship and the well-being of each partner improve as a result of their efforts. Even if a relationship ends, we want to feel we have made our very best effort to improve things rather than feeling regret over not having done more.

Many couples find that when their goals and intentions are aligned, the outcome exceeds their greatest hopes. They manage not only to stay together but to cocreate a partnership that far surpasses what they had previously shared or, in some cases, even imagined. Time does play an important role in the healing process, but it's not the only player. When we do our part and assume a proactive stance, things will inevitably shift, and often in ways that can surprise and even amaze us. You decide. Is it worth taking the chance?

Myth 11

You need to disclose all your past experiences in order to build trust.

The word *disclosure* gets tossed about in the context of relationships quite a bit these days. It's one of those terms that seem to arouse strong opinions. Some people believe that certain things are best left unsaid and that revealing so-called "unnecessary" details is just asking for trouble. Others believe that withholding *any* details about one's past or present is a form of dishonesty.

There is no rule about the "correct" degree of transparency in any relationship. While in general more is better, "more" doesn't mean complete or absolute. The degree of disclosure that each couple chooses to practice depends upon how they define it and what they agree to. Like many other practices, it's a matter of coming to terms with each other's point of view and creating a mutually satisfying agreement.

To begin, ask yourself as a couple: "What exactly do we hope to accomplish by disclosure?" It's up to each couple to determine this and to decide what is and is not relevant to the

relationship. Sharing every detail about routine shopping trips
probably isn't essential. On the other hand, if someone arrives
home three hours later than usual, asking where the person
was, is a legitimate question. Wanting to know about your
partner's past, recent as well as distant, is par for the course,
but each of us needs the freedom to keep some things private.
What we disclose has at least as much to do with communi-
cating what we are *currently* experiencing as it does with de-
scribing past behavior. Doing this requires each partner to
be self-reflective and self-aware. The ability to convey our
present-moment experience is vital to the quality of connection in any relationship. If I am feeling hurt or happy in response to something that my partner did or said, concealing or
denying that could negatively impact our relationship.

The issue of disclosure essentially has to do with honesty
and transparency. It's about promoting deeper trust, respect,
and integrity, and it's up to each couple to agree about what constitutes relevancy and importance. When there is a difference of
opinion, it's usually best to take the conservative path and go
with the partner who needs a higher degree of disclosure.

Trust-building doesn't necessarily require each partner to
confess all their embarrassing, uncomfortable, or shame-filled
experiences from the past. This perspective treats disclosure
as a kind of confession, with the hope that some degree of ab-
solution will be experienced by revealing these experiences. If
this is the case, then it's a good idea to disclose this motivation
to one's partner in order to clarify one's underlying intent.

Both giving and receiving information in the disclosure
process can be challenging, since this can sometimes activate
strong emotions in each partner. The person who is receiving information is challenged to be cognizant of their own

responses and to acknowledge them. This means saying, for example, "I felt jealous when you told me about speaking to your ex-boyfriend yesterday," or "Hearing you describe the way your father treated you made me feel sad for you and angry at him."

This kind of trust-building involves several elements: sufficient time to process the information, the capacity for self-awareness, and a shared appreciation of the value of this kind of rapport. Some of the payoffs of practicing disclosure include gaining a sense of ease and peace of mind that promotes greater security; greater closeness and shared intimacy; a feeling of being seen, known, and accepted for who we are, fears, flaws, and all; a feeling of freedom and safety to bring up any subject without concern about being judged or reprimanded; no longer feeling obligated to adopt a persona that conforms to the expectations of others; and letting go of the fear that "if my partner really knew me, they wouldn't love me."

When two people create a disclosure agreement, they open the door to possibilities that don't exist in relationships in which withholding or other forms of dishonesty are tolerated. This kind of connection doesn't happen overnight. Rather, it builds slowly, gradually, lovingly, and patiently over time. It begins with a willingness on the part of both partners to consistently engage each other with openness, authenticity, vulnerability, and honesty. This may seem like a tall order, but when you consider the benefits, it's a pretty low price for a great return.

Myth 12

Commitment and freedom
are mutually exclusive.

I f you believe that it's necessary to choose between a life of freedom and one of committed partnership, welcome to the club. What is often referred to as "commitment phobia" tends to arise when people believe it's necessary to surrender freedom to be in a committed partnership. To say the least, the idea of being trapped in a relationship from which there is no exit is an unappealing prospect. But is it really true that freedom and commitment are mutually exclusive, that it's an either/or proposition? While in many cases it's not possible to have it both ways, a great relationship is one in which having it both ways is not only possible but a requirement.

To begin with, we need to define our terms. "Freedom" refers to being unencumbered by restraints that limit our ability to take actions that fulfill our desires and needs. Having freedom means that we have the power to exercise the choices that we wish to make. Having that power doesn't necessarily mean that we will always opt for choices that fulfill our desires, since doing so would present its own set of problems. Most adults consider the consequences of their choices, or of acting on their desires, and they usually (but not always) make decisions that serve their well-being. This does not mean that we never opt for that second helping of pasta or dessert. But we have the freedom to make that choice if we want to. The more we are denied (or perceive that we are denied) freedom, the more compulsively we will crave that which is forbidden. This is the reason that diets often don't work. Even if we deny ourselves certain culinary delights, the sense of deprivation, of having our freedom to choose curtailed, can result in resentment. We become inclined to rebel against the alleged depriver, even if that person happens to be ourself. If we are in a relationship, and we perceive that our freedom to act is determined by our partner, or by a moral code that we don't fully accept, this sense of resentment and the impulse to rebel will be strong, and it will obscure feelings of appreciation and love.

Love without freedom quickly breeds resentment or claustrophobia, neither of which keeps the spark of passion alive. And freedom without someone to share it with simply isn't much fun. When asked what she most enjoyed about living alone, the celebrated French film star Jeanne Moreau replied that it was "the freedom to ask someone to share my solitude with me."

When we are without the security and safety that come with close relationships, our need for connection and intimacy gets neglected. In the most fulfilling relationships, both partners feel respected, trusted, loved, and free. The key to creating such a relationship lies in each partner becoming secure and self-accepting within his or her own skin. While to some this idea may seem unrealistic, if not impossible, many couples are living proof that freedom and love can coexist simultaneously. Love without freedom soon devolves into resentment, and freedom without love results in loneliness and isolation.

It's not possible to have a good relationship unless you have it both ways. The fundamental requirement of all partnerships is to honor the integrity of the relationship, which means to be willing at times to put the other's needs and preferences above yours *without* losing yourself and neglecting your own needs in the process. (Note that there is a significant difference between being *willing* to do this and always doing it.) It's likely that there would be a lot fewer marriages if more people realized how demanding the challenge of creating a mutually fulfilling relationship can be. Marriage certainly allows us to experience the joys and blessings of sharing life with a loved one, but many don't have a realistic awareness of what creating this involves.

The dance of love and freedom allows two people to open their hearts and experience deep intimacy without clinging or trying to control each other. The experience of separateness is as integral to this dance as connection. Relationships do require the willingness to give of ourselves in order to make adjustments to each other. But when we are fully aware of the benefits that deep connection provides, these offerings to our partner feel more like gifts than sacrifices.

One of the greatest gifts that this dance provides us is the experience of being truly seen and known as we are. When we feel someone's love and acceptance of us, we can begin to love ourselves more unconditionally. This provides a sense of freedom from the need for the approval of others, something that we crave when we don't possess self-acceptance.

Love and freedom aren't mutually exclusive; they are interdependent, two sides of the same coin. Once you experience the truth of that fact in your relationship, you'll never doubt it again!

Myth 13

Little things aren't worth getting upset about.

Charlie: "Take it easy." "Chill out." "Relax." "Lighten up." "Cool down." "Don't stress out." "You're making a mountain out of a molehill." "It's not a big deal."

These are some of the things I used to say when I didn't want to hear Linda's complaints, such as after I'd failed to keep my word regarding something I promised to do. Back in the day, this was, unfortunately, not infrequent. I'd fail to be ready to leave at a certain time to go to the airport, or I'd forget to pick up groceries on my way home, or I'd make other commitments for an evening that was meant to be our date night, or, well, you get the picture.

As much as Linda hated to be disappointed and upset with me, I hated to hear her grievances, even if they were provoked by my negligence. Partly, I didn't like feeling scolded for doing something wrong. For the most part, I knew that she had a right to feel the way she did and that I was guilty of dropping the ball. But hearing Linda's disappointment also put me directly in touch with her feelings, and it didn't feel good to know that I had something to do with them. Rather than acknowledge my guilt and the legitimacy of her feelings, which might have strengthened my motivation to make amends, I instead often chose to make excuses, or to explain or justify my actions (or inactions). I became defensive and told Linda she was making a big deal out of nothing.

I was a great believer in the notion that the best defense is a good offense. Linda was always quite offended by my efforts to turn the tables on her and make her feel wrong for being upset. She knew I did this to avoid dealing with or admitting the consequences of my own irresponsibility. The trouble was, as I learned the hard way, while this strategy might work in football and other contact sports, it fails miserably in the game of relationships.

It took longer than I would like to admit for me to finally get it. I tend to be a slow learner, but I did eventually learn. The "it" that I finally got was that it's not just *some* agreements that are important and need to be kept, but *all* agreements. You're not a bad person if you fail to honor your word, but there are consequences, even if what you've agreed to doesn't seem all that important, like handling the cat box by the end of the day.

The consequences of failing to keep agreements go far beyond the immediate situation. They extend into the foundation of your relationship. When one partner has a pattern of unfulfilled promises and broken agreements, trust inevitably suffers, as does the other partner's sense of being held in esteem. They will begin to feel, "I must not be that important to you if you constantly prioritize something else over me and the agreements that we make."

These feelings are compounded when the partner who has broken agreements is unwilling to accept or acknowledge the feelings of upset and disappointment that inevitably arise. The point isn't that we can never make mistakes. At times, we will drop the ball. But when each honors their word and takes agreements seriously, there is a much greater likelihood that mutual understanding and connection will be enhanced. With Linda, I realized that she was speaking up because she cared enough about our relationship to be honest with me when she felt let down or disappointed.

My offensive strategy had another unpleasant aspect to it, which was to discourage Linda from expressing her feelings to me out of a fear that in doing so she would be dismissed by me. Why would she want that? It would be easier just to stuff her feelings and tell me, "It's okay, I understand." The problem is that denied feelings have a way of turning into resentment. As they accumulate, unexpressed resentments have a way of turning into nit-picking, criticism, judgment, and passive-aggressiveness. Taking what looks like the path of least resistance in order to avoid conflict can in the end turn out to be the path of greatest resistance.

The little things count. If you have a habit of being late, being defensive, denying responsibility, or neglecting to keep your word, breaking that habit can seem like a daunting prospect. But take it from one who's been there, it's very doable once you get committed to doing it. And if you keep that commitment to yourself, you'll be much more likely to keep those commitments that you make to everyone else!

Myth 14

Relationships shouldn't have to be this hard.

One of the most frequent questions that we hear from people is, "Why does creating good relationships require so much work? If it's so natural for us to love one another, shouldn't it be easier than this?" In fact, I've asked the same question myself many times. The poet Rainer Maria Rilke, in his book *Letters to a Young Poet*, knew and acknowledged this truth when he wrote, nearly a hundred years ago, "to love another human being is perhaps the most difficult of all our tasks." Recognizing the degree of difficulty in this task is nothing new, but that still doesn't answer the questions of why exactly it is so hard and what the nature of the "work" is that we need to do in order to master this challenge.

It can be comforting to know that many others, even those who, like Rilke, possess great wisdom and spiritual strength, also share this experience. Yet despite the awareness that creating rich and rewarding relationships requires work, it's often easy to believe that, when things get hard, this must mean there's something wrong, either with me, you, or us. This belief is tempting because it provides an excuse for avoiding the work that relationships often demand. After all, there is no point in even trying if we're a bad fit, or if I'm just not suited for a committed partnership, or if you are too damaged or unwilling to do your work. So let's just end it and cut our losses, since this ain't gonna go nowhere nohow.

Then, perhaps we do end it, and we meet someone else with whom we think things will be different, and they are different for a while, until they're not, and the relationship suddenly requires work, and we repeat the same cycle all over again.

Sound familiar? You don't have to split up or divorce in order to go through this cycle. It's possible to recycle the whole pattern with the same person and stay together. It's just not a lot of fun. As many learn through experience, staying together provides no assurance that we'll be any happier than we would be otherwise. Even if we choose not to get involved with anyone ever again, those same issues that created suffering in a romantic relationship will come up in other relationships. Our hopes and wishes notwithstanding, we can't help but relate to others, since we are all at our core interdependent creatures. It's not possible for us to thrive or even survive outside of the context of relationships. We are destined to recycle our patterns until . . . we do our work.

What exactly does that mean? It means the following:

- Accepting responsibility for our own happiness and well-being and holding ourselves accountable for having gotten to the place where we are, and acknowledging our intrinsic capability to affect change in the quality of our own life experience.

- Letting others off the hook and releasing them from our belief that it's their job to make us feel the way we want to feel, and it's their fault if we don't.

- Forgiving those who have disappointed us, let us down, hurt us, or betrayed us in some way.

- Forgiving ourselves for all the unskillful choices we've made, unkind acts we've committed, and unwise options we've taken.

- Becoming willing and able to live more openheartedly, and providing ourselves responsible security and self-care when we need it.

- Making and keeping a commitment to our own integrity and understanding what that really means.

- Recognizing that our partner isn't necessarily as demonic as they may seem even when they are at their worst, and that we are not as innocent as we believe ourself to be, even when we are at our best.

- Assessing our values and making sure that we are living by what we say matters and being honest about what we really care about.

- Transforming our resentment and self-pity into empathy and compassion.

- Feeling gratitude that we have awakened enough to know what our work is, that we have the motivation to do it, and that we are not alone in accepting the challenge of becoming a more loving human being.

- And being very, very patient and reminding ourselves that this is the work of a lifetime, not of a weekend or a month or even a year, and that it's not about getting the job done. Rather, it's about staying committed to the process and trusting that staying on the path is the reward that we get for our efforts.

Perhaps it's less important to know exactly why relationships often require hard work than to know that you're not alone if you feel this way; in fact, you're in good company. However, you probably won't get to see who else is on the path until you're on it yourself.

It's been said that you get what you pay for, and there's no doubt that great relationships require the payment of some dues. Whether you choose to ante up is up to you. As Linda likes to say, "It's not a 'have to,' it's a 'get to.'" You get to make this choice because you're already awake enough to see that you have a choice to make. Congratulations.

Myth 15

All the good men/women are taken.

Linda: We have heard vast numbers of people make this claim over the years. I try to keep my mouth shut when I hear it. I usually say something like "It only takes one, you know, but you may have to kiss a lot of frogs." It certainly can be quite a process to find an eligible player for a good relationship. I'll be the first to acknowledge that there are some trials and tribulations to go through. It's not easy to find somebody who will pair up with you, who will make a contract to support your development, who won't bail when things get hot, who can stand the heat, and who will join you in embracing relationship as a path to greater awakening.

Given the challenges involved, why *would* you want to go through this demanding process? Isn't it easier and less stressful to save yourself the trouble and stay out of the game altogether? After all, if there's nobody out there who's available, who's really somebody worth being in relationship with, then why even try?

Many people espouse this belief because it spares them the need to risk becoming emotionally involved with others, thus eliminating the possibility of experiencing rejection or disappointment. It's based on the assumption that beyond a certain age, everyone who is a qualified candidate for a committed relationship is already taken, and the remainder of the playing field consists of losers, users, and liars. Those who hold this position have a tendency to collect "evidence" from others who feel the same way, and thus affirm this view. The perspective that the situation is hopeless justifies the avoidance of emotional engagement, and it protects someone from the risks inherent in starting new relationships. Romance is replaced by a network of friends with whom one can commiserate and find solace and sympathy.

Qualified, decent, worthwhile, eligible potential partners do exist out there. Whether you live in Manhattan or North Dakota, whether you're nineteen or ninety, whether you're a conservative or a liberal, whether you like country music or classical, whether you are gay or straight, there are people with whom you can create true partnership. What it takes is this:

- The willingness to risk involvement.
- The intention to commit to *becoming* the partner of your dreams, rather than trying to *find* him or her.
- The willingness to hang in there without getting discouraged, even if it means you have to kiss a few frogs.
- The ability to be selective about who you talk and listen to, and to pay less attention to nay-saying friends and more attention to the ones who know otherwise.

- The intention to do your own work to become a more loving, authentic, and trustworthy person.
- And the patience, trust, and faith that make it possible to enjoy the ride between now and the time that you get to disprove this belief!

Myth 16

Nothing good can come from conflict.

Conflict in relationships has gotten a pretty bad rap over the years and for good reason. Unresolved differences are the source of a lot of physical, mental, and emotional distress. Many couples find that arguing is painful, and they decide that it's better to avoid acknowledging differences at all. Some couples have made explicit or implicit agreements to deny differences that could potentially activate hurt feelings.

This policy may be an effective short-term strategy, but it can have disastrous long-term consequences if used on a regular basis. When differences aren't adequately addressed, there is a strong likelihood that withheld feelings will morph into slow-burning resentment, ongoing frustration, emotional disengagement, depression, or worse. Ironically, it's often the desire to prevent damage to the relationship that motivates the impulse to ignore differences.

A "take no prisoners" attitude can be harmful and should

be avoided. If avoidance doesn't work either, what do we do? Fortunately, these two options are not the only ones that are available. A third possibility is to engage in what we refer to as "conscious combat." Conscious combat is distinct from what is commonly known as "fighting" in the following ways:

FIGHTING	CONSCIOUS COMBAT
One relates to the other as an adversary	One relates to the other as a challenger
The intention is to defeat "an opponent"	The intention is a mutually satisfying outcome
The focus is almost exclusively on differences	The focus is on shared interests
Uses coercion and manipulation	Uses direct, open, and honest behavior and communication
Views differences in terms of right and wrong	Willing to acknowledge areas of difference without judgment
Focus is on getting the other person to understand or agree	Focus is on understanding the other's perspective
Intention to be heard	Intention to listen
Intention to protect	Intention to connect
Intention to repress	Intention to express
Intention to conceal	Intention to reveal

While conscious combat is much more likely to produce a mutually satisfying outcome than simply fighting, admittedly it is not an easy strategy to practice. We have all learned ways of managing differences, most of which contain serious downsides. The lessons of painful conflicts can often lead us to avoid the vulnerability that conscious combat requires. Letting down the protective armor of our defensive strategies can seem risky and dangerous. Yet practicing vulnerability and emotional disarmament is more likely to produce a conciliatory response than defensiveness, which often invites aggression.

Standing undefended in the face of a perceived threat is not for the faint of heart. It requires courage, dedication, and practice to cultivate the qualities of a conscious combatant. But the benefits of mastering the art of conscious combat extend far beyond enhanced effectiveness in conflict management. The expression of grievances can illuminate what's missing or not working for one or both partners. When we can express and receive this input through effective forms of communication, we can more easily reconcile differences through the open exchange of concerns, needs, and desires. As this process continues, mutual understanding and appreciation grow.

When couples start to practice the principles of conscious combat, it's generally best to begin by addressing smaller concerns that are less emotionally charged. Try to be patient with the process. It's easy to forget how entrenched our defensive patterns often are. It's not surprising, since we've been perfecting them for years, even decades. Simply deciding to interrupt them with new practices isn't likely to bring immediate and permanent change. But it may be enough to begin a shift that, with perseverance and intentionality, will bring about profound results. It's been said that living with an open heart requires a cup of understanding, a barrel of love, and an ocean of patience. Sometimes that seems like an understatement.

Myth 17

True lovers feel love
for each other all the time.

Linda: Years ago, when our kids were small, one scenario played out again and again between Charlie and me. It had to do with my wanting connection and Charlie being distracted and unavailable to be present with me. These situations would often deteriorate into conflict, since neither of us was particularly skilled at handling our differences. Usually this occurred when Charlie returned from one of his frequent work-related trips, which often took him away from home for a week at a time. By the end of the week, I would be hanging on by my fingertips, barely able to keep it together, and counting every moment until he walked through the door.

Unfortunately, when Charlie finally did walk in the door, he was often so emotionally and physically burned-out that the last thing he wanted to do was to have a deep, meaningful, sustained connection with me. He had just spent the past week working fourteen-hour days in intense interactions with dozens of people. He had been barely holding it together until he was able to make it home and recover in what would sometimes be as little as twenty-four hours before his next trip.

Having been with people all week, Charlie needed some quiet time and solitude, which ran directly counter to my need for connection. Now, having him finally home, but being unable to be really *with* him was almost more painful than being separated. The lack of connection felt unbearable, and his lack of availability seemed a confirmation of my suspicion that he didn't really want to be with me. By my reasoning, if he did, he would feel like I did and would want to rush into my arms and melt into me.

This pattern of reentry was a source of great suffering for both of us, and we struggled with it for a long time. I came to fear and dread our reunions, but neither of us saw any hope that things could substantively change, at least as long as Charlie kept his job. And he was clear that he wasn't willing to consider leaving it.

The problem wasn't just the reentry process, but it was our inability to get beyond the frustration and anguish that we both felt and reinvigorate our emotional connection, which was in need of replenishment after several days of neglect. We needed to get caught up, but we never seemed to get there.

Charlie: The pattern was always the same: I'd come home and get rushed by the kids, who would hug my legs and wrestle me to the floor, where we would all roll around and laugh until I broke free and went over to Linda, who had patiently and graciously stepped back to allow them to have their piece of me first.

Linda: I knew that they hadn't seen Charlie for a week and that they weren't able to defer their desire to play with him as well as I was. But still, a voice inside my head asked, "When is it going to be *my* turn?" and "Why do I always have to be last?" But it didn't seem right to get mad at our children, so I was conflicted, and my inner conflict always ended up playing itself out between me and Charlie.

Charlie: I was in a quandary, too. I really did want to be with Linda and hated to see her unhappy, but I knew that if I didn't get some cool-down time alone in my study, I wasn't going to be much fun for anyone to be with. I felt guilty for not being able to be there with Linda and angry at myself for not being a "bigger" person. That didn't really help very much.

Linda: Both of us were bringing mixed feelings that were obscuring the love that was underneath them. To me the scariest thing in the world was when I felt disconnected from Charlie's love. At those times I would go into a panic and get demanding and angry, which are feelings that Charlie, understandably, wouldn't find particularly attractive.

Charlie: And I would respond accordingly, by getting angry and shooting back pretty ugly words that were designed to get Linda to back off and shut up. It wasn't a pretty picture.

Until one day we had an interaction that changed things permanently. The interaction went like this:

Charlie (immediately after walking into the house): Hi, Honey. Hi, kids. Daddy's home. (Kids run in and wrestle Charlie to the floor.)

Linda: Where were you? Your plane got in almost three hours ago.

Charlie (defensively): It took a long time to get my baggage, and the traffic out of the airport was horrendous. You

wouldn't believe it. Oh yeah, I stopped by the office to file
my expense report, since if I didn't, I wouldn't be able to
do it for two weeks...

Linda: You've got time for the kids, time for your expense re-
ports, time for everything and everyone but me! Don't
you know that I've been handling everything here alone
all week, and we have barely even spoken on the phone
since Tuesday! Sometimes I wonder why you ever got
married! You don't even love me, do you? (Crying.)

(Charlie groans.)

Linda: See! You can't even tell me that you love me. That
proves that you don't. (Now crying really hard.)

Charlie: Wait a minute. Can I answer your question?

Linda: What question?

Charlie: About whether I love you.

Linda: I know the answer. Your silence spoke volumes!

Charlie: Please give me a chance.

Linda: Okay...what?

Charlie: I do love you. Really. But I hate it when we have these
fights. I hate it because when we fight, I don't *feel* loving toward you. I feel hurt, I feel angry, I feel scared, I
feel frustrated...and those feelings obscure the love that I
have for you that is always underneath them. So do I love
you? Absolutely. I want us to be together always, and I
have no plans to ever go anywhere. And do I always feel
that love at a deep level? Not always. Sometimes I don't.
And when you ask me for reassurance of my love at a time
when I'm feeling any of those things that I just mentioned,
in that moment I can't tell you what you want to hear and
mean it. But that doesn't mean that it's not there. Sometimes I just have trouble accessing certain feelings because

I'm distracted or preoccupied. But the love is still there, and I can usually reconnect with it if I can just get myself centered and disconnect from those other distractions. Can you understand what I'm saying? Do you believe me?

Linda (long pause, then quietly): Yes. I believe you.

Charlie: Thank you. (Long pause.) I hate it when we fight. I hate being out of touch with my love for you, and I hate knowing that it's not just you. I realize that I play a big part in these breakdowns that are so painful. I get angry at myself whenever you are disappointed in me because I feel like I've failed you and let you down, and then I get mad at you for "making me feel bad." Crazy, isn't it?

Linda: Thanks for clarifying things. I'm glad that I'm not the only one who hates our fighting and that you don't see me as the problem because I get so distraught when there's a disconnect between us. Maybe I'm kind of crazy myself, but I can't help it. Our relationship is the most important thing in my life, and when we're not in sync, it's hell. And when we're connected, it's heaven.

Even though we love our partner, there will inevitably be times when we do not feel that love to the same extent that they do. A myriad of factors influence the degree to which we are in contact with loving feelings. Understanding this fact can enable us to find the patience and trust to forgive ourselves and/or our partner during the times when those feelings aren't present in our experience.

Paradoxically, accepting the absence of loving feelings in certain moments can actually reawaken them. Feelings such as hurt, fear, anger, loneliness, and jealousy can override our softer, more vulnerable emotions, often causing us to doubt or question love. While feelings of love are not always consistent and present, love itself can be deeper and constant, even during those times that it is not felt. The more true to ourselves and each other that we can be, the more present those loving feelings will be between us. When we trust the truth of our own love, we trust the truth of our partner's love, we trust that we are deserving of that love, and the doubts and fears dissolve and disappear. And it just doesn't get much better than that.

Myth 18

If you really loved me,
I wouldn't have to ask.

ost people don't believe that it is reasonable to expect others to read their minds, but that does not always stop people from becoming hurt or angry when their partner doesn't. When it comes to intimate relationships, many believe mind reading is a legitimate expectation. Holding this view frees us from having to directly express our withheld needs and desires. This expectation can, as we usually find out the hard way, lead to (ahem) "difficult" situations.

The following re-created dialogue between Karen and her husband, Peter, offers an example of what it can sound like when one or both partners fail to fulfill the unspoken expectations of the other. After Karen arrived home from work, Peter greeted her and was met with cold silence.

Peter: Is anything wrong?
Karen: Why? Do you care?

Peter: What do you mean? Of course I care. Karen, what's the matter?

Karen: You know I had tests done at the doctor's today.

Peter: Yes, I know. How did it go?

Karen: If you do really care, you sure have a strange way of showing it. You never called to ask me how it went, and you know that I was very worried about this test.

Peter: I did call and you weren't available, so I left a message.

Karen: Right. You called once and left a ten-second message. You didn't try very hard to reach me. One call! If you really cared, you would have called back. I really needed you, and you weren't there. I knew I couldn't really count on you when I needed you. (She begins to cry.)

Peter (becoming angry): I'm sorry that you feel uncared for, Karen. I can't always know what you need or expect from me. I made an effort to reach you. I guess that wasn't enough, huh? (He shakes his head, throws his hands up, and walks away.)

If you've ever been on either side of a scenario like this, you're not alone. And you know how it feels — not particularly good for either partner. The accuser often feels abandoned and unloved, and the accused may feel shamed and often becomes defensive or angry. This is a prescription for conflict and possibly gridlock. Unfortunately, these interactions occur all too frequently because of our tendency to make assumptions and hold unspoken expectations. Many of these are based upon culturally sanctioned myths. "If you really loved me, I wouldn't have to ask" is one of them.

Accusations like this are often made in an effort to avoid vulnerability or rejection. We often hear from people, "But I shouldn't *have* to ask for something that should be naturally provided by someone who loves me." To this we say: Perhaps it's true that your partner doesn't love you and doesn't want you to feel cared for and appreciated. It is, however, also possible that your partner has other reasons for not responding in the way you wanted in this situation, and it isn't because he or she isn't a genuinely loving person. Examples of some of these reasons include:

- You each have different understandings of what constitutes "sufficient" effort to accommodate a perceived need.
- Your partner would not feel the way that you do if they were in your situation.
- Your partner gave you what they would want if they were in your situation.
- Your partner was preoccupied with something else in that moment.
- Your partner hasn't stopped loving you, but they were just having a bad day and so weren't available for you in the way that you hoped for.

Another explanation is that your partner may actually *not* have felt loving toward you at that particular moment. Feelings of love are not constant, and they are sometimes interrupted by other emotions and concerns. If there are patterns of consistent negligence, disrespect, or callousness, there may be reason for concern and doubt regarding a partner's degree of caring. Still, a failure to mind read does not constitute legitimate grounds for an accusation of being unloving.

In cases where there is concern regarding the quality of a partner's feelings, there are other, more effective ways of dealing with the situation than by projecting accusations. Doing so only increases the likelihood that each partner will become defensive, which is like pouring gasoline on a fire.

Failing to express specifically what we want or need can be a defense to avoid being vulnerable. It can feel safer to criticize our partner than to acknowledge certain desires we have, particularly ones we fear they may not fulfill or even respect. Expressing in very specific, rather than global, terms the nature of those desires helps minimize the likelihood that our partner will feel attacked. Seeing beyond our hurt or frustration to identify our unmet needs can require focused effort, but naming these desires and then expressing them to our partner in a respectful, nonjudgmental way will create a very different outcome than the scenario that Karen and Peter experienced.

Some examples of unfulfilled desires include wanting the following:

- More recognition or acknowledgment
- More emotional, physical, or sexual intimacy
- More solitude
- More caring and attentive listening to our concerns and ideas
- More help with the housework and/or childcare
- More time together to address "unfinished business" and other issues
- More fun and play time together

These are just a few of the unexpressed needs and desires that can be neglected when we fear the consequence of bringing them up. Even couples who have been together for decades don't possess the ability to read each other's minds. It's impossible to ever know another person that well. There is, fortunately, always room for surprises in relationships. As the old saying goes, when we assume, we make an *ass* out of *u* and *me.* Arrogance is thinking that we know something to be true when it may not be. The antidote to arrogance is humility, and that requires the courage to risk vulnerability and emotional honesty.

That may sound like a lot, and in fact, it is more than many people are up for. But for those who are, the payoffs far outweigh the risks. More often than not, the feared consequences of expressing our needs don't occur, and we are relieved when things turn out differently than we had anticipated. Some surprises are quite delightful. But don't take our word for it. Try it and see for yourself.

Myth 19

Love will heal my past emotional pain.

C had had all the features that were on Miranda's perfect partner checklist: he was intelligent, financially fit, good-looking, and athletic, and he loved kids and cats. So why, she wondered, did she always feel as if there was something missing or not quite right between them? Miranda often felt that Chad was trying to control her, even though when she confronted him with her feelings, he insisted that he wanted her to be free to make her own choices and do what she felt was right for her. While Chad sounded sincere, Miranda never felt that she could really trust his words, and she had a large collection of "evidence" that she had gathered over the three years that they had been together. In her mind, this evidence "proved" that he was determined to direct her life. When Chad suggested that they move in together, she became so fearful of the possibility of losing control of her life that she insisted that they would need to get counseling together. Without that, she couldn't trust that her fears would not become a reality. Chad agreed and reassured her that he had no intention of trying to pressure her into doing anything against her will.

Chad: I told Miranda that I wasn't interested in making her into someone other than who she is, but she continued to be suspicious of me. She needed a lot of reassurance that I wasn't going to put a collar around her neck and put her on a leash like a pet. I asked her to give me a chance to show her that I wasn't a controlling guy.

Miranda: Part of me really wanted to move in with Chad, but I've always been sensitive to issues of control, and another part was terrified of giving up control over my own life. I had spent a lot of my life feeling like I wasn't in charge of my decisions, but my parents were. I wanted Chad to not only take away my fear of being controlled but also make up for all those years in which I had to be the perfect child. My parents had such rigid expectations of me that I was in a constant state of tension. I couldn't make a wrong move, get my clothes dirty, speak too loud, or get anything less than straight As in school.

Through Chad's support, I've come to realize that I had been holding some very big and unrealistic expectations that were impossible for anyone to fulfill. Prior to that I had been very disappointed and angry with him because he wasn't fulfilling them. I had been hoping that Chad would take away my fear and all that distress that I had been carrying for years from my suffocating childhood. There were and still are many things that he can and does do that help. He likes having us both included in making important decisions, and he asks my opinion about things rather than acting unilaterally. The evidence was coming in, but I was still so scared. It finally dawned on me that it wasn't up to Chad to take away my fear of losing my freedom and being controlled. It was up to me to draw my boundaries clearly, and also to learn how to relax them from time to time, so that I wouldn't turn into a hyper-controller myself.

Chad: I couldn't rescue Miranda from having grown up so straitjacketed in her childhood, but I could and wanted to support her to find out who she is and to live her life as that person. I give her a high five when she takes some chances, tries new things, or sticks up for herself when she and I don't see things eye to eye. I really want her to feel that she can do things her own way and that I don't love her any less.

Miranda: Chad didn't rescue me from the pain that I brought into this relationship, but he did show up with love and support while I figured out how to live my life according to my own script. That has made all the difference in the world, and for that I will always be grateful.

To the degree that early unhealed wounds and unmet childhood needs are carried into adulthood, we may see our partner as having the power, even the responsibility, to rescue us from the residual pain of these experiences by providing us, finally, with the quality of love that we had never received. What we deeply desire is love that is healing, affirming, redemptive, and unconditionally accepting — in short, salvation. Not only is this expectation unrealistic, it's unattainable. Still, the desire for love is so compelling that it frequently blinds us to the reality that may conflict with these longings.

When we lack a sense of wholeness, we often seek out a

partner whom we hope will fill our emptiness, someone who seems to possess the power to restore us.

Such a person often inflames the desire for redemptive love, the kind of love that can heal our hearts and souls, not just make our bodies feel good. When we are redeemed, we feel "right" with ourselves and relieved of feelings of unworthiness, doubt, anxiety, and shame. "This time," we tell ourselves, "this person will love me in the way I really need and deserve to be loved, and their love will remove all the pain from my life."

This is the redemptive longing, the hope of being saved once and for all, perhaps because we feel ourselves to be unworthy of real love, which is by nature unconditional. If we fail to recognize the illusory nature of this expectation, all too often relationships that begin with dreams of divine bliss deteriorate into unrelenting frustration and bitterness. The person whom we had hoped would be our salvation becomes the source of excruciating emotional pain because, being mortal, they are unable to fulfill our desire for consistent unconditional love.

Once we see the true source of our attraction and our attractiveness to others, we begin the real healing work that can free us from relational patterns that no longer serve us. With this awareness, we can learn how to put out the fires of suffering at their source. When we do this, we diminish the inclination to compromise ourselves in order to gain love from others. Looking for wholeness and security through another is like seeking relief of a toothache from a painkiller without getting the necessary dental work done. It will temporarily alleviate the pain, but it is not an effective long-term solution.

The source of the problem is an unwillingness to honestly

face ourselves, in particular those parts that are in need of attention and healing. This process involves the ability to recognize who we really are and claim all those parts that compose the fullness of our being.

This doesn't necessarily require us to reveal our deepest, darkest secrets to the world, but simply to honestly acknowledge the truth to ourselves. When we do this, over time those aspects of our personality that we may have tried to conceal become exposed to the light of awareness and compassion. This process of gradual awakening, both to ourselves and to others, is the essence of the work that will set us free. This freedom is the foundation of a fulfilling relationship and a fulfilling life.

Myth 20

You can be right
and have a good relationship.

The key word in this myth is *and*. While many of us may claim to believe that the need to be right and a good relationship do not go together, we act as if the opposite were true. While we claim to recognize the danger in insisting that our view is always the correct one, we nonetheless act as though we can get away with indulging our desire to be right without jeopardizing our relationship. When we truly recognize that being right and having fulfilling relationships are mutually exclusive, the impulse to attempt to coerce our partner into seeing things our way diminishes and the desire to understand the other's perspective becomes more dominant.

Wanting to be right is a form of defensiveness. Resisting the impulse to act defensively is easier said than done. All types of defensiveness have to do with implementing different types of control. Defensive reactions include (but are not limited to) withdrawal, blaming, interrupting, counterattacking, guilt-tripping, justifying, explaining, invalidating, intimidating, rationalizing, pleading, and cajoling. Trying to be right is a strategy to invalidate another's perspective in order to have our own point of view define the "reality" of the situation. When we feel provoked or criticized, particularly by someone with whom we have an intimate relationship, this impulse to be right or act defensively can be strong. It may seem out of proportion to the situation. This can happen when someone's words or behavior activate our unhealed emotional wounds. When our "hot buttons" are triggered, we can be possessed by emotions that we usually keep beneath our conscious awareness through a range of protective mechanisms. Unfortunately, we pay a price for keeping these feelings outside of our awareness.

Our resistance to experiencing unwanted feelings diminishes the quality of our relationships and inhibits our capacity to experience intimacy. It blocks our creative energy and causes us to live with pervasive low-level anxiety. Contrary to popular advice, it's usually not possible to simply "let go" of the past. Until we identify the roots of our defensive patterns, we continue to be enslaved by them. The best way to recognize what we need to see, but have been avoiding, is by being in a close relationship. Committed partnerships by their very nature activate our deepest longings, strongest desires, greatest fears, and most intense emotions, primarily because we pin our greatest hopes on these chosen partnerships. Consequently, when we feel disappointed by our partner, the pain can be overwhelming. One of the ways in which we may attempt to avoid or mitigate this pain is by trying to control our partner's behavior. Being right is one way of trying to fulfill that intention.

Freeing ourselves from the need to be right and from the

grip of defensiveness is not so much about changing our behavior as changing our perspective of a given situation. Differences in perspective are inevitable in all relationships, and they are valuable. They remind us that there are other ways of viewing things. There isn't necessarily a single "truth" that must be determined and held by everyone. If we believe there is only one correct viewpoint, we will feel the need to "correct" our partner rather than accept and come to terms with our differences. Such corrective actions inevitably result in heightened defensiveness on both sides, and before you know it, we're off and running.

The habit of defensiveness is not one that easily dissolves, even when we possess a commitment to neutralizing our old reactive buttons. Knowing what we "need to do" is not always enough to make us do it. Our conflicting desires — such as to be in control, to seek approval, to protect ourselves, to be right — often override our willingness to be vulnerable, honest, and transparent. Yet despite these concerns and conflicting desires, it is possible for anyone, or any couple, to interrupt the defensive patterns that tend to show up. Yes, it does take effort and courage to expose our vulnerable emotional underbelly in the face of fear. But regardless of the outcome, in the process we can become more loving and lovable, and this greatly enhances our ability to create the relationship of our dreams.

Myth 21

After I'm married,
I won't ever be lonely again.

Mira and Joel got together when they were both in their early twenties. They shared this story with us thirty years later. By that time, they had grown children and were enjoying a deeply loving marriage. As their story suggests, it was not always blissful for them along the way. Confronting their illusory beliefs proved to be a greater challenge than either of them expected. But as they discovered, the outcome was well worth the effort and time the process required.

Mira: When I fell in love with Joel, I had the romantic notion that he would rescue me from my lifelong unhappiness, and I would never feel lonely again. I had grown up as an only child, and I was not close with my parents. I spent a great deal of time alone and longing to be seen and heard.

Joel: I grew up with three siblings, and since my family never had much money, the six family members had to squeeze

84

into a tiny apartment where I couldn't get any privacy. After I left home and Mira and I moved in together, I found myself desperate to finally create some private space for myself. My efforts activated Mira's fear of abandonment, and we hit some very rough times early on.

Mira: To me, when Joel took time alone, it triggered the old pain of being left by myself, with all those old feelings of not being important, valued, and loved. It was as if I were a small girl of about four years old, and I had fallen into a well. I felt so helpless and hopeless down there in the well of grief that I didn't even bother to yell for help. I didn't think anyone would bother to lower a rope down for me to escape. I would just get quiet and feel the old pain of aloneness.

Joel: I would eventually notice that Mira was silent and withdrawn. By that time she would usually be weeping, and it was impossible for me not to notice. We made a pact that she wouldn't expect me to read her mind and recognize that she needed connection. She promised to let me know when she was suffering, so we could connect before she fell back into the well.

Mira: Our agreement was a big turning point for me. Rather than being in the disempowered position of waiting for Joel to notice, I began to act like a grown-up, rather than a neglected child, and ask for what I needed in the moment. I gave up my romantic notion that Joel would take away all my suffering from my awful childhood. Now I often turn to my women friends for connection and attention so that I don't burden Joel with this need. The amount of connection I need in order to thrive is too much to ask of any one person.

Joel: Ironically, since Mira has given up her romantic notion
that I will redeem her from her childhood loneliness, she
tells me that a great deal of that sadness has faded away.

Mira: I have worked long and hard to build a rich, active support network. So nowadays, I spend very little time down
at the bottom of that dark, gloomy well. Most often, I can
prevent myself from falling in by staying connected to my
friends. When I do fall in, I speak on my own behalf and
ask for help, either from Joel or one of my friends, and that
has made all the difference.

Feeling alone and unsupported reinforces mistrust, which
can cause us to blame our partner for not making us feel more
secure. Many of us believe that our partner should be all things
to us and meet our every need. This is an impossible expectation for one person to fulfill.

Getting together with friends, inviting guests to share dinner, creating a neighborhood party, singing in a choir, joining
a book club or bowling league, participating in group dancing or community theater, showing kindness to a stranger, and
doing something for the good of the community are all examples of ways to fulfill our emotional needs.

In the face of life's challenges, the best thing we can do is
to make our little corner of the world more safe, welcoming,
friendly, kind, caring, and loving. When we take good care
of ourselves by strengthening our friendship network, it puts
us in a positive frame of mind, which has a direct beneficial
effect on our romantic partnership. In accepting responsibility
for providing for our own personal and interpersonal needs,
we are not burdening one person with that obligation. Being

part of a robust community inevitably enhances our primary relationship.

We are not in the community to get support; we are in the community to exchange support. We contribute to a shared purpose, and when we are focused on something outside of our own personal desires, some of those other personal concerns like loneliness become less significant and fade into the background. A community can be as small as a couple of people, or it can include thousands. When we are part of a group that embraces a shared commitment, whether it's two people or two thousand, loneliness can't really be sustained in the presence of that interdependence. It's the ultimate win-win game.

Myth 22

Commitment means
staying together no matter what.

It's not surprising that many people have mixed feelings when it comes to taking on a commitment. The term *commitment* includes the ideas of irrevocability, entrapment, permanence, and loss of freedom. One definition of *commitment* is "official consignment, as to a prison or mental health facility; the state of being emotionally or intellectually devoted, as to a belief, a course of action, or another person." Is it any wonder that so many of us have some degree of "commitment phobia"?

Of course, there are other, more positive definitions of commitment, such as "pledge, vow, assurance, giving one's word, empowering, investing, entrusting." One way or another, a commitment can be a powerful vehicle to support the transformation of our lives. While marriage vows are meant to be permanent, we would like to offer another take on the word *commitment* that provides a little more breathing room without compromising the word's essential meaning, particularly in regard to relationships.

A commitment isn't simply a promise that relates to time and longevity, but it defines the nature of that promise. Commitments are made outside of time. Our commitment defines the kind of relationship we are agreeing to cocreate with our partner. It takes into consideration the following questions:

- What is our shared purpose in coming together?
- What is our vision for the future?
- What experiences can we create together that we can't achieve alone?
- What do we see in each other that makes us want to spend our lives together?
- What will each of us do to help our shared aspirations come to fruition?
- And are we both willing to hang in there to do what it takes even when things get tough?

Commitment can be seen as an agreement to deal with the challenges and opportunities that relationships inevitably provide. It is the container that holds our sacred pledge to fulfill what we see as the fundamental purpose of our connection. It is a context that can hold inconceivable possibilities for our lives and the lives of everyone we touch. Any intentions or goals that two people hold can be included in this container. Those goals can be as specific and personal as intimacy and self-discovery, or as universal as service to a cause or to a shared honoring of a spiritual tradition. We all determine the nature of the contents of our container.

When we remember that no one but ourselves has the authority to hold us to a commitment, it no longer feels so confining. True commitments cannot be assigned by another; they must spring from within the depth of our own heart. When this is the source of the commitment that joins two people, they will not feel forced to stay together, but they will feel blessed in the gift of their partnership.

There will be difficult times. Even the best relationships have their moments (and longer) of hardship, suffering, and doubt. Being committed doesn't prevent these experiences from arising, but it reminds us that our underlying shared intention is bigger than the temporary distress that we may experience from time to time. It reminds us that these bumps in the road are opportunities to engage in practices that strengthen the qualities that support us in becoming more whole and loving human beings.

Over the course of a relationship, doubts and difficulties can cause us to question whether it's really worth it to continue to hang in there. It's possible to be committed and to simultaneously confront this question. Commitment doesn't mean that you now have to sleep in the bed that you made (so to speak) for the rest of your life, no matter what. But it does mean that you both share an agreement to honor the principles of your contract. In getting married, you aren't agreeing to a "life sentence" but to a "shared vision." Marriage provides a container that concentrates and focuses a couple's shared commitment. This agreement deepens the feelings of mutual trust, motivation, and safety that are necessary in order to do the work of strengthening the relational bond.

A commitment is more than a single promise. It's a structure that holds a number of different skills, qualities, and practices, including communication skills, negotiating for our needs, managing differences effectively, practicing cocreativity, and responding to opportunities and challenges that are inherent in relationship. The real power in commitment comes from our willingness to continually choose to honor it. In this process we align and mobilize our energies together in order to fulfill our shared vision. Like electricity, commitment is a force field that can be used to bring about any outcome. At its essence, it is neither positive nor negative.

Committed relationships call forth the best and the worst from us, from the ecstatic passion of infatuation to the pain of conflicting desires. Breakdowns are inherent in the process as we pass through various stages of relationship, but these provide us the means through which we can open to deeper levels of our heart's greatest longings.

Unique opportunities exist in committed partnerships, some of which include a heightened experience of joy, generosity, creativity, and passion for living.

As a wise man once said, "There's no free lunch." Committed partnerships do not come cheaply. They require courage, responsibility, imagination, and integrity. Very few of us enter these relationships fully developed in those areas. It's mostly on-the-job training. But with a vision, a spirit of adventure, a willingness to play your edge, a willing partner, and support when you need it, the possibilities are endless!

Myth 23

Telling the truth means getting it all off your chest.

Charlie: For the first few years of our relationship, Linda and I were believers and advocates of the theory that the way to deal with anger is to express it directly and clearly to the person you are upset with. This provided me with a very convenient justification to rationalize my inclination to convert all my more vulnerable emotions (like fear, disappointment, sadness, shame, desire, and so on) to anger and to unceremoniously dump them onto Linda. Since I was quite a bit more experienced and comfortable blaming, shaming, and raising my voice than she was, this worked pretty well for me. At least it seemed to until Linda let me know that it wasn't working so well for her.

Linda: Charlie came from a family in which it wasn't just okay to blast people with your anger, it was considered a legitimate way to deal with all sorts of emotions. Not only was he comfortable venting his anger on me, he felt completely justified in dumping his judgments and criticism on me as well, claiming that it was for my own good, insisting that I needed to develop a thicker skin and get over my fear of other peoples' disapproval. I know that it sounds crazy, but for a long time I bought into the rationalizations that he used to justify his tendency to indulge his temper.

Charlie: It's not easy to admit it, but I was nothing more than a bully. I was picking on someone who was no match for my skillfulness in projecting punitive anger and whom I assessed as unable to stand up to the heat of my accusations and as unpracticed in the art of manipulation by intimidation.

Linda: Unlike Charlie, I grew up in a family where the children were punished for expressing anger toward anyone, particularly adults. Arguing or even talking back to a parent could easily result in a severe and painful punishment. There was zero tolerance for any expression of anger or even defensiveness. I learned that if I were to survive, I would have to become a master at concealing any feelings that could provoke reactivity in my parents.

Charlie: In graduate school in the seventies, Linda and I were exposed to a school of thought that came out of the encounter movement in which the notion of venting negative emotions on others was seen as therapeutic and beneficial. This gave further legitimacy to what had by now become a dysfunctional pattern of hostility and defensiveness in our marriage.

Then I got a job facilitating personal growth workshops in which "catharsis," which literally means "a purifying cleansing of the emotions by bringing forth repressed feelings," was an underlying principle of the seminars.

Linda: By this time, having survived a great many encounters with Charlie, I had overcome enough of my fear of confrontation that I was willing to stand up to him rather than allow him to intimidate me into submission. While this was definitely a step in the right direction, it was by no means a solution to the impasse that we had come to in our marriage. It had become overwhelmingly obvious to both of us that our policy for dealing with our differences was clearly not working and that we were dangerously close to losing our marriage. With good professional guidance, we learned that openheartedness and vulnerability produce a very different outcome. We soon began to climb out of the abyss that we had fallen into years ago. Since then, not only have we put the painful past behind us, but we've experienced a degree of trust and goodwill in our marriage that goes far beyond anything that either of us had ever imagined.

Charlie and I personally learned the hard way that projecting anger onto others is never productive. We have since recognized scientific research that affirms the conclusions that we arrived at from our own experiences.

One of the researchers, Russell Geen, author of the book *Human Aggression*, found that while "blowing off steam" at someone may temporarily calm an angry person, it is also likely to amplify underlying hostility and may provoke retaliation and escalation. According to Geen, repeated expressions of intense anger toward another don't lessen violence or neutralize strong emotions; instead, they lower social inhibitions against the expression of violence. People become more likely to engage in additional verbal violence. Also, after the projection of anger, these feelings are frequently replaced by anxiety and guilt, trading one unpleasant state for another. Letting off steam often makes people angrier, not calmer. Those who indulge in venting toward another person may have a large amount of repair work to do after a hostile encounter. It can take several days, or longer, to repair the damaged trust and to establish the feelings of safety, harmony, and respect that allow love to flow freely.

Still, despite ample evidence to the contrary, the "catharsis hypothesis" continues to have appeal. Many people see only two options: express hostility or stuff it. Neither of these choices are productive strategies for conflict management. A better solution would be to turn down the heat by expressing feelings without hostility, blame, and faultfinding. Instead, seek to create an outcome in which both parties are satisfied with the result rather than one in which there is a winner and a loser. Anger need not be denied or withheld but, rather, expressed without accusation or an intention to punish or retaliate. In this way, there is a much greater likelihood that an open and respectful dialogue can occur, making it possible to address the underlying causes of the disagreement or misunderstanding. This solution requires assertiveness rather than aggression, and it prevents feelings of guilt, anxiety, and fear from escalating.

Charlie: Linda and I did eventually learn what it takes to be more emotionally honest and vulnerable. When we did, we were able to communicate in ways that defused our reactivity rather than intensified it. The very things that had previously activated intense arguing no longer set us off.

Linda: One example of how we handled things differently occurred when Charlie forgot our date, and instead of getting angry and blaming him, I chose to get vulnerable and more emotionally honest. As you will see, this led to a very different outcome. Here is a re-creation of that conversation:

Linda: I'm really hurt and disappointed that you forgot. It seems like it isn't important enough to you to remember our agreement. It means a lot to me that we keep these dates, and I'm afraid that they mean a lot more to me than they do to you.

Charlie: I'm sorry. I feel an urge to explain why I forgot, but I know that's not what you need to hear right now. I can see how you'd feel that way. I know that I have a tendency to get distracted and that I can get forgetful and neglectful of things that are important to me. I'm not excusing or justifying my forgetfulness. I hate it when I let you down and cause you to doubt that you are valued by me.

Linda: I'm glad to hear that, but I need to know that these dates are important to you, too.

Charlie: I know that, and they are. I don't always like to admit it, but I need them as much as you do.

Linda: It's really good to hear you say that. What is it specifically that you need me for?

Charlie: Yeah, I know that I don't talk about that very much, but since you asked...I need the reassurance that you give me of your love. I need the care that you show me in your interest in how I'm doing. I need the acceptance that I feel from you when I have self-doubts. And I need our shared physical closeness.

Linda: Thanks for the reassurance that you need me. And I need all those things, too. Right now, I'm feeling valued and important, and that feels great!

Charlie: Thanks for being patient and giving me reminders when I need them.

Linda: You are very welcome.

Vulnerability is disarming and much more likely to promote deep understanding and reconciliation. If that is your goal, give it a try. Or you can keep fighting. It's your choice.

Myth 24

Love means never having to say you're sorry.

reakdowns happen in relationships. Despite our best intentions, we will at times be careless with words, hurt our partner's feelings, unfairly displace anger, do or say things that we regret or that cause harm, and more. This is not to excuse such transgressions, but to acknowledge the inevitability of these situations. It is a good idea to do everything that we can to minimize the frequency and severity of our transgressions, but when they do occur, the next best thing is to minimize damage. This process generally involves repairing the trust that has been broken.

While sometimes a simple apology may be sufficient to restore goodwill after a breakdown, in many cases, particularly those in which there has been a more serious upset, it will require more than "I'm sorry" to restore goodwill.

A sincere apology involves more than making a statement of regret over having caused pain. It's a good beginning, but it will generally require more than this to complete the process.

An effective apology requires several components in order to repair a relationship breakdown. These include the following:

Intention: Get clear about your intention before you even begin the conversation, and stay true to it. This will help keep you from getting sidetracked by distractions that inevitably come up in heated conversations. Remember that your job isn't to prove that you're right but to demonstrate that you can be trusted to listen nondefensively and respectfully to your partner's feelings and to show that you truly care about your partner and what they have to say.

Acknowledgment: Be willing to recognize that there has been a breakdown.

Responsibility: Accept your part in the breakdown. This is not to be confused with blame or fault. It has to do with acknowledging that you may have acted or spoken in ways that diminished trust, respect, or goodwill.

Sincerity: A sincere apology is one in which the speaker has no agenda other than to heal whatever damage may have occurred as a result of his or her actions or words. The words need to be spoken with honesty, with genuine heartfelt feeling, and without an intention to coerce, deceive, or manipulate the other person's emotions.

Nonreactivity: Exercise restraint and patience as you talk about the issue. Resist any temptation to "correct" your partner's version of the scenario or argue with their perspective or feelings. This is an essential aspect of the healing process. Your partner may have a lot of emotion to express, including feelings that may have to do with other, previously unacknowledged disturbances. Give your partner a chance to speak without fear of reprisal. This demonstrates that you really *do* want to listen and that you're not just there to be heard. Keep in mind that silence does not equate with agreement. Just because you are not arguing with someone doesn't mean you're necessarily seeing everything their way; rather, you're simply giving them a chance to express their perspective.

Curiosity: Be curious rather than adversarial. Find out what your partner needs from you in order to find resolution. Don't assume you already know. Even if your partner does not tell you anything that you don't already know, your sincere *interest* in their needs will communicate the kind of caring that they need in order to begin to trust you again.

Keep in mind that reconciliation is a process, not an event. Don't be too quick to ask for forgiveness. Your partner may experience this request as just one more thing that you are trying to get from them. Your partner probably will need more time than you think they "should" in order to adequately process their feelings and get complete.

Apologies can be and often are an essential part of the process. While the words of your apology are important, equally important, if not more so, are the behaviors that you demonstrate during and after the apology. As the saying goes, talk is cheap. Actions really indicate a person's true intentions. There's a difference between talking the talk and walking the talk. The key to effective apologies is the depth of your sincerity to embody your words and show your partner that you have learned and integrated some critical lessons.

Apologizing gets easier with practice; many of us get plenty of opportunities. Each opportunity can strengthen the qualities that great relationships require, including compassion, vulnerability, patience, commitment, and intentionality, to name a few. In the process, not only might you restore love and goodwill, but these might improve beyond what they were before.

Whether that happens may have more to do with you than you think!

Myth 25

There's just not enough time.

Jason and Carolyn are a power couple. He's an investment banker, and she's an attorney. They also have two daughters, ages seven and five. They have a commitment to provide quality parenting for their girls and share child-rearing responsibilities. In between jobs and childcare, they somehow manage to squeeze in regular workouts at the local gym. They also are on several community and neighborhood committees and volunteer at their daughters' school. In their spare time, they... well, there isn't much of that. Unfortunately, there isn't a lot of time or energy left over for much of anything else, including their love life, which is the real neglected child of the family. To say that the romantic element of their relationship is in the toilet would be a gross understatement. By the time they collapse into bed at night, they have barely enough energy left to turn out the lights. And sex? What's that? If they make love once a month, it's a minor miracle.

Things, of course, were not always this way.

Jason: Before we had kids, it was all very different. We both knew that there would be changes after the kids came along, but neither of us ever imagined the degree to which we would feel overwhelmed with all the demands of fulfilling the needs of the family, our marriage, and ourselves.

Carolyn: I've always been blessed with a strong constitution that has allowed me to burn the candle at both ends and accomplish as much in one day as any three people. I thought I'd be able to overachieve forever. Boy, was I wrong! But we've created a lifestyle and added new commitments that require a lot more from us than we seem to have time or energy to provide. I'm not sure how it happened, but all of a sudden Jason and I found ourselves with much more weight on our shoulders than we could carry, and it's really hard to see what we can put down.

Jason: I was brought up to believe that you eat your vegetables first and clean your plate before you can have dessert. In my mind that translates into fulfilling your responsibilities first and then you get to play and have fun. The problem is that it seems like the vegetables keep getting piled onto the plate, and it never gets clean. Consequently, playtime never happens. And all work and no play makes Jason an unhappy boy.

Carolyn: And it makes Carolyn an unhappy girl. Neither one of us has been a lot of fun to be around lately. I don't even like being around myself these days. I used to have a great disposition, but now I find myself grumbling to myself and to whoever else will listen about how burned-out I'm feeling. I know that we need to do something about how overcommitted we are, but I just don't see how or where the changes can come from.

In a marriage, the couple's relationship is the hub of the wheel of the family, from which all other parts of our lives radiate like spokes. When the wheel is out of balance, things don't run smoothly. Our capacity to manage stress diminishes, and the smallest difficulties can seem insurmountable. When the hub is strong and the wheel is balanced, even the biggest challenges become manageable.

Jason and Carolyn are not lacking in intelligence or motivation. What they are not doing is directing their attention to the area that will bring about the greatest return for their energies. That's right, their relationship. This is not a matter of "working on their relationship"; it's about feeding the relationship and giving it the time, energy, attention, care, and pleasure that it requires in order to thrive. And how, one might ask, is it possible to add another plate to the twelve that are already spinning? The answer is what we refer to as the "Bic cure."

The Bic cure is writing in ink (unerasable) on your calendar a weekly date night or afternoon, with frequent day-long getaways. Nowadays, many people use their electronic devices to schedule important appointments. Both methods work. Carolyn and Jason need to have reliable, consistent, trustworthy childcare to be responsible for their kids during the times that they are giving care and nurturance to the other child in their family, their marriage.

For the Bic cure to be successful, it's necessary to schedule romantic interludes and commit to them. Writing in ink on a calendar is one way to treat them as permanent. Since time spent on the health and maintenance of your relationship is as essential as any other aspect of your life, this time must be held as sacred. The dates are just as important as any client appointments, dentist visits, or pediatric checkups. As Carolyn and Jason regularly nourish their parched romantic partnership, it will plump up and spring right back into shape.

Jason and Carolyn both accepted the "Bic challenge," and while Jason was optimistic and enthusiastic about trying out this idea, Carolyn was somewhat hesitant and protested that she liked spontaneity. Scheduling took some of the fun out of it. But Jason suggested that scheduled intimacy time didn't preclude the possibility of spontaneous interludes, and it might even make them more likely. At first she was reluctant, but Carolyn agreed to give the Bic cure a try, and guess what? Her fear that scheduled intimacy time would be mechanical and unexciting proved to be unfounded. "Once we got into it, I was amazed at how much I enjoyed being close again. I hadn't realized how long it had been since we'd shared time together that didn't involve conversations about work, kids, or money. It was less about the physical connection that we shared and more about the feeling of being close and free from concerns about the responsibilities that prevent us from really being with each other, in the truest sense of the word. I felt like someone who had been dying of thirst who was finally getting a long drink of cool, refreshing water."

To follow the Bic cure, it is inevitable that we will have to draw boundaries and say no to some professional opportunities and to some social engagements. But it is for a good cause. Our family and friends will just have to understand the importance of prioritizing our romantic partnership. And when we take care of our primary relationship, it grows healthy, strong, and beautiful, just as our children do. The benefits in having a deeply fulfilling connection with each other extend far beyond the relationship itself. Our health, career, financial well-being, relationships with family and friends, creative expression, and even spiritual life all radiate out from the well-being of our flourishing partnership. As these outcomes become manifest, and you begin to reap the benefits, you won't ever complain about not having enough time to nurture your love together. That's a promise.

Myth 26

When it comes to togetherness in relationships, more is always better.

There's not much question that many relationships suffer from a deficiency of quality time together, a condition that greatly diminishes the experience of connection shared by a couple. Other responsibilities and commitments have a way of winning the competition for our time, leaving us feeling resentful, frustrated, tired, lonely, or some combination of the above. While insufficient connection time is unquestionably a common phenomenon that afflicts many relationships, it is by no means a universal condition; in fact, some relationships have the opposite problem. They don't have enough separate space, and this can cause a different but no less serious problem for the couple. In his book *The Prophet*, Kahlil Gibran reminds couples of the importance of including separate times as well as connection in a relationship:

But let there be spaces in your togetherness,
And let the winds of the heavens dance between you.

Love one another but make not a bond of love:
Let it rather be a moving sea between the shores of
    your souls....
Sing and dance together and be joyous, but let each
    one of you be alone,
Even as the strings of a lute are alone though they
    quiver with the same music.

In most relationships, one of the partners is more attuned to the need for separateness, while the other has a greater awareness of the need for connection. Differing tendencies can create some "interesting opportunities" for learning and growth for both partners. The differences can provide a means of integrating both separateness and connection in a way that fulfills each of these needs. The challenge is to see each other's perspective as being legitimate, and even necessary, and not condemning it as wrong.

When one or both partners are not experiencing enough solitude, certain symptoms are likely to show up in mood and behavior. These symptoms include crankiness, irritability, lethargy, volatility, anxiety, depression, and fatigue. To correct this, begin with the recognition that times of solitude or separateness are called for. Solitude is distinct from isolation, as they have different intentions. Isolation may be involuntarily imposed, and it is characterized by an inability to make sustained interpersonal contact. We seek isolation when our intention is to disconnect from others to *avoid* experiences we expect will be unpleasant, threatening, provocative, or difficult to deal with. Solitude, on the other hand, is motivated by a desire to recharge one's spiritual and emotional batteries in order to more effectively *engage* with others and with the world in general. Consequently, isolation tends to strengthen feelings of resentment, self-pity, defensiveness, and mistrust. Time spent in solitude deepens our capacity for self-awareness, compassion, empathy, and vulnerability.

Solitude is a state of being in which one has voluntarily chosen to be alone. The desire for solitude can be driven by a variety of intentions. We might want to be alone in order to read a book, watch a movie, take a drive, or walk on the beach. Or we might focus on meditation, prayer, and deliberate self-reflection, in which nothing else is "done" except contemplation. Even a few minutes of solitude can be enough to freshen your perspective, but if there has been a prolonged solitude deficiency, a personal retreat of a weekend or more could be necessary to begin the restorative process.

Introverts might embrace the chance to feel "unburdened" of the "responsibility" of having to deal with others' needs, whereas extroverts might feel less attracted to solitary experiences. But everyone needs some solitude in their life in order to strengthen the capacity for self-reflection, even if they aren't consciously aware of it or have no interest in being quietly alone and introspective.

Solitude is a form of self-care. For many people it may not feel particularly comfortable to be alone without the usual forms of distraction (phones, computers, television, books, other people, and so on), but the experience of taking the time to recharge our inner batteries and shift our current mind-set to a more open perspective can be both valuable and necessary.

Most people need to address certain logistical challenges

in order to disengage from their primary commitments in a responsible way. Because Western culture tends to highly value interpersonal interaction over contemplative time, it is easy to judge oneself or others as being antisocial or isolating, when this isn't necessarily the case. If we internalize those cultural assessments, we may fault ourselves, or our partner, for having the desire to periodically detach.

If we give in to this attitude, we might deprive ourselves of this experience and fail to meet this need. Eventually, our physical or emotional health, or our relationship, might break down. Honoring our need for solitude doesn't guarantee that such breakdowns will never occur, but it helps us handle them when they do occur. We can correct problems more quickly, and damage can be minimized.

Sometimes, one partner is more able and willing to create times of solitude than the other. This can cause envy, disguised as criticism or resentment, in the other partner. If one partner is taking an excessive amount of time to be separate, or using this time to avoid the other, there may be legitimate grounds for concern and the issue should be addressed. Solitude time may need to be negotiated until an adequate degree of trust is developed.

More together time can be the answer to many relationship difficulties, but this is not necessarily a one-size-fits-all solution. Nor is it always the case that couples need to spend more time in separate spaces. Relationships, like all living organisms, are in a constant state of flux, and consequently, they require ongoing attention, care, and tweaking. Taking time to be apart from each other occasionally, with the intention of engaging in the kind of self-reflection that isn't available with another person, helps us identify and address the questions that may be invisible to us when we're caught up in life's ongoing demands. Giving yourself solitude time isn't selfish; it's the most generous and respectful thing that you can do for yourself and everyone else that you care about. See for yourself!

Myth 27

If you don't have something nice to say, don't say anything at all.

No one likes to be the recipient of bad news, particularly when it's about themselves. We don't like to be confronted, even in a nice way, for being the cause of someone else's distress or failing to keep an agreement. Many of us also have a strong tendency to withhold giving input to others that we fear may cause them to feel upset or angry. We are reluctant to say things to others that aren't "nice," perhaps out of an awareness that, if we do, they will be more likely to reciprocate in kind. Consequently, we may adopt some effective ways of discouraging negative feedback or invalidating such feedback when we receive it.

While this strategy may protect us from receiving messages that we'd rather not hear, there is a downside to it. When we prevent the messenger from giving us the message, we deny ourselves valuable information about how we come across to people and how they respond to us. Our self-assessments aren't necessarily the most accurate portrait of how others see us. There's a world of difference between being open to hearing the experience of others and feeling compelled to win everyone's approval.

Here are some examples of responsible feedback: "I was disappointed when you didn't keep your agreement to follow up on the project that we've been working on." Or, "When you didn't show for our meeting, I became worried that something had happened to you, and I thought that perhaps I had written the wrong time in my appointment book." Or, "I got angry at you and quit talking yesterday when I felt frustrated with your continual interruptions when I was trying to speak." Or, "I'm noticing that I'm less trustful that you'll keep your word, since the last four times that you've promised me that you would do something, you didn't do it."

It's hard when someone whose opinion of us matters expresses mistrust, disappointment, anger, or other negative emotions. When we minimize or diminish the legitimacy of another's feelings by justifying our behavior or telling them that they are making a bigger deal out of something than it is, we let them know that we are not receptive to their feelings and that we don't respect their concerns. It doesn't take many responses like this to stop the other person from sharing any thoughts or feelings that they fear may trigger defensiveness. The consequence is almost always a diminishment in the level of trust and respect in the relationship.

At one time or another, most of us have been on both sides of this kind of situation. As you probably know, dismissive responses generally *are* very ineffective strategies for getting the job done, that is, if the "job" is to discredit the other person's perceptions by making them wrong for feeling the way they do and for honestly expressing themselves to you. This in no

way is meant to suggest that one should tolerate disrespectful reactions or unsolicited criticism from others. Responsible
feedback expresses one's own feelings in an effort to help and
to fix a problem, but not everyone has this goal. Delivering
unwanted advice, judgments, blame, or condemnation of another is something else altogether.

According to author M. Scott Peck, in his book *The Road
Less Traveled*: "A failure to confront is a failure to love." Although there is a lot of truth in what Peck says, more often
than not our defensive attempts to silence someone who is giving us difficult feedback are driven by a desire to prevent our
image from being tarnished. The bottom line is that we don't
want to look bad, to ourselves or to others. And bad is how we
think we will look if we're caught in the act of being unreliable
or insensitive. When our actions reveal unattractive aspects
of our personality — because we used angry or disrespectful
words, engaged in hurtful behaviors, or violated a trust — it's
natural to want to explain or justify ourselves in order to avoid
the shame or embarrassment we feel. "Shooting the messenger" isn't necessarily the best way to deal with someone who
is bringing us this news; however difficult it is to accept, such
information is worth listening to. Sometimes we may not be
aware of our transgressions, and even if we are, we may not
want to be made aware of how it has impacted another person.

While reacting defensively with hostility or judgment
when confronted with someone's feelings may intimidate
that person into shutting up or retracting their words, there
is a downside to winning that game. These feelings don't go
away; they go underground, below the surface of awareness,

and they will arise from time to time in various forms, directly or indirectly expressing themselves.

Consequently, when couples find themselves arguing over topics like money, sex, kids, and in-laws, these subjects can be cover-ups of the actual concerns. Often underlying these symptoms are issues of power, control, respect, trust, freedom, or acceptance.

When it comes to dealing with broken agreements or with emotions that arise between people that need attention and understanding, there is no such thing as "no big deal." Any disturbance that is unacknowledged or unattended *is* a big deal, and it quickly becomes a bigger one if it is denied or invalidated.

Confronting our partner with honest feedback requires both courage and sensitivity. It's not just a matter of speaking the truth of our own experience, but more importantly, expressing it in a way that is respectful and responsible. That is, without blame, judgment, or accusation. When we do this, there is still the possibility that they may respond with defensiveness or anger. These feelings can, however, be dissolved through continued constructive dialogue, and in the process the relationship will be strengthened. When we withhold our truth, this impacts the integrity of the relationship, and this will put us on a very slippery slope downward.

As we learn to be both respectful and honest in delivering news that isn't easy to give, and to be open and nondefensive in receiving that news, we not only preserve the integrity of our relationship, but also deepen the level of trust that we share.

Managing the emotions that inevitably arise when we really listen to each other's concerns requires tolerance and restraint. It's in the crucible of relationships that we find the motivation to strengthen these and other personal traits and qualities, and in the process we open the possibility of shifting the trajectory not only of our relationship, but also of our life. And that *is* a big deal!

Myth 28

It's too late to bring it up now.

There is no statute of limitations when it comes to unfinished business. When a breakdown in a relationship remains unresolved, regardless of how long ago it occurred, it's never too late to address the issue.

Not that bringing it up will be easy. Many people feel that after some (unspecified) amount of time passes, certain subjects become off-limits. Any attempt by one partner to revisit an issue can trigger a refusal to reengage with the subject. The person may say, "That's history," "We already discussed this," "You should have said this yesterday when we were having the conversation," and, "It's too late to bring it up now." Most of the time, the person is trying to avoid a difficult or uncomfortable conversation. But this is ultimately counterproductive, since refusing to acknowledge and deal with an unresolved issue will inevitably result in amplifying an already aggravated situation.

One of the things that couples with great relationships

have in common is a shared commitment to talk about any concern that feels unfinished with either of them, regardless of whether or when it may have previously been addressed. Refusing to revisit unfinished business denies us the opportunity to become free from the heavy feelings that often accompany unresolved issues. Sidestepping potentially painful subjects can sometimes be a convenient justification to avoid risking emotional upsets. In doing so, we create a potentially greater risk: the likelihood of diminishing the levels of trust, respect, and goodwill in the relationship.

We often hear people say that they don't have enough time to talk anymore. A more honest response might be: "The last thing that I want is to talk about my feelings or to hear about yours."

Another reason people may resist dealing with unfinished business can be a fear that the subject is being brought up with the intention of using it to blame, criticize, or shame the other person.

There may have been a good reason for feelings to have been stashed in the deep freeze, particularly if there was a painful disconnect in the first place. It's always a good idea to examine one's purpose in bringing up a previous issue. If the intention is to learn from the experience and create greater mutual understanding in order to finally lay it to rest, revisiting the concern is more likely to bring a more satisfying outcome than an intention to punish or fault the other person. A positive intention to complete unfinished business can help reassure one's partner. An example of this could be: "My hope in having this conversation is that we may both feel closer to and more understanding of each other and learn something that can enhance the quality of our relationship."

Janet hit an impasse with her husband, Wendell, when she tried to talk about a recent incident that involved her in-laws. By clarifying her intention and stating her feelings without blame or judgment, Janet was able to express her desire for Wendell's involvement in a way that he could join her in her concerns.

Janet: Your parents called to invite us to come to visit next Sunday. I'd like to talk about our last visit to their house when they were rude to me.

Wendell: This is old news! Why are you bringing it up now? That was a long time ago. If you had something to say about it, you should have said it at the time. Nothing can be done about it now. We should be looking ahead to the future.

Janet: I am looking ahead to the future, and that's what I want to talk with you about, but I can't just forget about the past. It's still bothering me. I was hurt about how they ignored me. The last time that we were all together they devoted all their attention to you and never even acknowledged me.

Wendell: But why do you insist on bringing it up now? Don't live in the past. It's over. Just let it go.

Janet: You're right; it would have been better if I had made more of an effort to include myself in the conversations or taken you aside to tell you privately how upset I was so you could help somehow. I didn't, and that's my fault. That's why I want us to get clear about what will work for me, how we can both set things up so that we don't repeat what happened then. I have some ideas about how we can prevent a similar situation from reoccurring, and I think that it will be a win-win for us all. I'd really appreciate your willingness to listen to what I have in mind and to work with me on this. Are you willing to do that?

Wendell: Well, I guess so. Yes.

Janet: Thanks. It really means a lot to me that we're on the same page, and if we work together on this, I know that things will turn out very differently than they did last time.

The incident that was bothering Janet may have been old, but when we don't address grievances when they occur, we can carry the feelings for months or even years. Even though the incident itself is over and in the past, the residual discomfort is alive in our present experience. Unfinished business doesn't disappear when it's not addressed, and it diminishes our sense of personal and interpersonal well-being.

In this case, Wendell's insistence that Janet "just let it go" represented an attempt to avoid the possibility of activating a potential conflict with his partner. Until Janet felt heard and understood, and both of them learned how to make the visits to the in-laws work for them, the issue would be a chronic irritant.

When issues are left unaddressed and incomplete, the levels of goodwill and trust in the relationship fall. In this case, Wendell did finally change his mind because Janet persisted in her efforts to let him know how important it was to her; she also needed him to help her cocreate a plan that would work for everyone. Because Janet presented her concerns with clarity and without blaming Wendell, and because he was open to hearing and responding to her hurt feelings, not only were they able to finish some unfinished business, but they brought a heightened degree of mutual respect and goodwill to their marriage.

Wendell pledged to make a committed effort to include her in conversations with his parents during their visits, and Janet promised to make an extra effort to include herself if she felt excluded, rather than withdrawing in resentment. Not surprisingly, the next visit went without a hitch due to their preplanning and cooperation.

When there is a painful emotional charge related to a past incident, it's never too late to bring it up. When we begin with a conscious intention to heal the damage and restore trust and harmony, we're already more than halfway there. When breakdowns are responsibly addressed, regardless of when they may have occurred, the outcome can not only restore our relationship to its previous point, but can bring us both to a greater level of mutual appreciation. So what are you waiting for?

Myth 29

Love and good sex will make your relationship affair-proof.

A lot of people who hold this belief have been deeply disappointed to discover that it's not true. This myth is deeply embedded in our culture and is even held by a fairly large number of marriage counselors. It just seems like common sense that if two people love each other and have a mutually satisfying sexual relationship, then there would be no reason for either of them to stray. Well, that is true. There is no good "reason" for that to happen. Affairs, however, are generally not motivated by reason or rational thinking. They tend to be matters of the heart, which is the source of passion and desire, not the mind.

It doesn't seem logical that partners in a happy relationship would be motivated to go outside the relationship to fulfill their most intimate desires, particularly if they've made an agreement to be monogamous. Yet it happens, and more often than most of us realize. Still more surprising is that according to relationship and sexuality expert Esther Perel, author of *Mating in Captivity*, the motivating drive to have an affair isn't the desire for sex. For most people, it's the desire for experiences that they are no longer finding in their primary relationship. What they desire, according to Perel, is attention, novelty, adventure, vibrancy, aliveness, and passion. They crave the experience of losing themselves in the intensity of the excitement and stimulation of a new relationship, with the hope of reinvigorating the feelings that occur in a state of infatuation.

When daily routines and responsibilities dominate the attention of one or both partners, the risk of a violation of the monogamy agreement increases. When either partner feels that they must submerge aspects of themselves in order to maintain peace or avoid conflict, the risk factor is similarly heightened. The fantasy of being free to be fully authentic, and to experience aspects of oneself with someone other than one's partner, is a compelling motivator for someone who has felt that they need to withhold or conceal parts of themselves in order to avoid judgment or rejection in their primary relationship.

The expectation that one person can and should meet all of one's needs, particularly when many of those needs are seemingly at odds with each other — security and adventure, excitement and peace of mind, spirituality and sensuality, tenderness and strength — sets us up for the likelihood of disappointment or resentment. This is not to justify violating one's marital vows, but rather to be mindful of the dangers of holding our partner responsible for fulfilling a range of needs and desires that are beyond the capacity of any one person.

Sometimes we may feel so heavily burdened by our obligations to earn a living, provide for the family, and bring up the children that an affair seems to promise a reprieve from a life of relentless responsibility. When partners take each other for granted and neglect their relationship, they put it in jeopardy. When unresolved conflicts mount up, resentment, anger, a lack of respect, and even contempt may form conditions that are an accident waiting to happen. Such animosity can provide a perfect rationalization for going outside the marriage for intimate contact.

Infidelity can be as brief as a single encounter that turns into a one-night stand or a years-long affair. Some may justify their indiscretions with the defense that there was no actual bodily contact, but even emotional affairs, where sex has not occurred, can damage the primary relationship. Each couple has the responsibility to come to an agreed-upon understanding of the kinds of actions that they see as constituting acceptable behavior within their relationship.

No matter what their cause or nature, every betrayal does damage to a relationship and always requires repair work, that is, if both partners agree to repair the relationship. Another statistic cited by the study in the *Journal of Marital and Family Therapy* was that only 31 percent of marriages lasted in which an affair was discovered or admitted. The shock of the crisis can expose the source of the unmet needs that the affair was an attempt to fulfill. In doing so, it can open the possibility for the breakdown to become a breakthrough, provided both partners do the work that is required of each to heal the relationship. Pain can sometimes be a great motivator.

It would, of course, be much more efficient to avoid the torturous stages of wounding and healing that accompany unfaithfulness. There are many things that can enhance the quality of your relationship. If you don't know what they are, ask your partner, and it's likely that he or she will be happy to give you a few examples of what you might do that could enrich the quality of experience for you both.

In the process of attending to your relationship, don't make the mistake of neglecting to nourish your own life. The juicier you are, the more attractive you'll be to your partner. Maintaining a vibrant life isn't selfish; it's a gift not just to you but to all your loved ones as well. Staying vital and alive and not going on cruise control is probably the best insurance for minimizing the chances of either of you having an affair. Love and good sex are great. By all means cultivate them both. But don't forget to keep your own spark alive by living your life with passion and purpose.

As the saying goes, an ounce of prevention is worth a pound of cure.

Myth 30

Marriage is a fifty-fifty proposition.

President Calvin Coolidge famously once said, "The business of America is business." Exactly what he meant by that has been debated for nearly a hundred years, but one thing that he most certainly did not mean is that the business of relationships is business. Living in a competitive culture, as we do, can promote a commercial orientation in all areas. It prompts us to see relationships as quid pro quo exchanges. Instead of giving our emotions and time freely and less conditionally, we often invest, expecting a return, and feel resentful if we aren't adequately compensated according to our expectations. Conducting a relationship as a business deal will get you in a lot of trouble. While we expect fairness and reciprocity, running our relationship like an accountant can engender mistrust and suspicion. When mutual trust is absent, serious difficulties can arise.

Consider the predicament of Laney and Jordan.

Laney: In the beginning of our relationship, I was a very efficient scorekeeper and kept careful track of who did what for whom. Fairness has always been a big deal for me. My stance was often, "If you give me this, I'll give you that." It drove Jordan nuts.

Jordan: I let Laney know, in no uncertain terms, how offensive this was to me.

Laney: My fear was that if I stopped keeping score, our relationship would become horribly lopsided, and I would be exploited.

Jordan: I was fearful that Laney's micromanagement of the score sheet could break us up. It drove me crazy dealing with her review of the balance sheets. I don't think good relationships should require that level of oversight. But apparently Laney didn't see things the way I did. We were locked into polarizing positions on this issue. It was very painful.

Laney: I now realize that my position seemed extreme to Jordan, but I was determined to make sure that no one would ever take advantage of me like my dad did of my mom.

Jordan: I realized that there was a line that I had to draw to stand up to Laney. The shift was gradual but powerful. It took several months, but the goodwill began to grow.

Laney: The result turned out to be the opposite of what I had feared. Jordan became even more generous than he had previously been.

Jordan and Laney stayed in dialogue, and out of their on-going exploration, they both became aware of how focused they were on each other rather than themselves. Jordan came to realize that standing up to Laney would require him to be willing to risk activating her anger, something that he had previously been loath to do. Laney recognized that much of her mistrust of Jordan was driven by her past experiences rather than Jordan's behavior. She saw that she had to be willing to take the risk of becoming less suspicious and more vulnerable.

Committed relationships are partnerships, and they require reciprocity. Yet keeping careful track of each other's contributions doesn't strengthen trust, it diminishes it. Of course, every household has to handle its own economics, and we have to create agreements related to who will earn how much, who will pay what bills, and whose life energy will accomplish what tasks. But when the interpersonal and emotional side of a relationship is carried on like a series of business transactions, there can be a tendency to withhold in response to feeling controlled.

When the flow of mutual giving stops, both people suffer. Feelings of hurt and deprivation lead to what world-renowned relationship expert John Gottman refers to as the "four horsemen of the apocalypse": criticism, defensiveness, contempt, and finally stonewalling. This downward spiral can spin out of control with potentially disastrous consequences if it is unchecked.

A relationship is much more than a business. We are wise when we relegate those businesslike parts of a relationship to a lower level of significance. We can instead work to cultivate more mutual generosity and trust. When couples are in the rhythm of giving, they are sensitive to each other's needs, and they get great pleasure from bringing happiness to each other. There are a great many forms that these practices of devotion can take, including loving touch, gifts, words of affirmation, and acts of service. Our greatest joy comes not from getting what we want but from seeing the delight in our partner's eyes when they receive our offerings.

When we last saw Laney and Jordan, Jordan said, "These days each of us is filled with so much gratitude that we both knock ourselves out trying to find ways to make the other person happy." And Laney told us, "At first it felt like a huge risk, but the outcome was much better than what I had feared it might be."

When generosity comes from a pure heart, both giver and receiver are beneficiaries. This is the essence of what is referred to as enlightened self-interest. It often does take a leap of faith to give up the scorekeeping and become less conditional in our giving. Of course, there are no guarantees regarding the outcome, but to say that it's worth the risk is a monumental understatement!

Myth 31

People don't change.

If we had a nickel for every time we heard those three words, we'd be rich.

The problem with this widely accepted cultural belief is that it's not true. Change doesn't necessarily happen in the ways and for the reasons we expect. And if it doesn't, it's easy to conclude that change can't happen. There's something attractive, even compelling, about believing that making substantive changes in our lives is unrealistic or even impossible. Believing that people don't change supports a worldview that justifies resignation, passivity, and helplessness. This state provides a rationale to avoid taking the risk and making the effort to be proactive and initiate change in our own lives. As with many other myths, the purpose of this belief is to insulate us from the dangers inherent in a life characterized by proactivity, risk, and vulnerability.

On the one hand, everyone has intrinsic characteristics or personality traits, such as being introverted or extroverted, analytical or intuitive. We may not be able to change these predispositions, but we have a great deal of power to influence them. We don't choose the traits that we are predisposed toward, but we can choose what traits we reinforce through our practices.

Changing conditioned patterns is not easy, but it *is* possible. Trusting this possibility requires us to give up our excuses for being the way we are. Only then can we fully commit ourselves to this transformative process. This is what we mean when we use the term "doing your own work." It is also a prerequisite to finding the motivation to "be the change" that you wish to see in the world. Motivation, or "intense desire," is a determining factor in this process. When it is strong, the likelihood of a positive outcome is great. When it is weak, the prognosis for success is slim to none.

To change, we must clearly recognize the benefits of putting the time and energy into the process. Since it's natural to expect desirable results from our efforts, we need to answer the question "What's in it for me?" Self-interest has to do with getting our needs met and our desires fulfilled, but if acting in selfish ways isn't working, we need to do something else. *Enlightened* self-interest is the awareness that when I change to behave in ways that contribute to the lives of others, my quality of life is also enriched. In a relationship, shifting from self-interest to enlightened self-interest not only changes the dynamics of the relationship but also fuels change within both partners.

People who have poor relationships are frequently acting out their fears and anxieties. How that manifests in their behavior runs along two major lines. The avoidant style is characterized by acting out a craving to feel safe, and people respond by withdrawing from the relationship and having minimal involvement. The controlling style is characterized by manipulation with anger, aggression, threats, and ultimatums. Some unskillful behaviors that result are using silence to punish, making critical or judgmental remarks, or being bossy by giving commands. Both of these styles reflect a resistance to change because the partner fears that any change may provoke undesired consequences. Both of these reactions are driven by the fear that any change could be a change for the worse.

Motivation to change can be strengthened by recognizing the effect certain behavioral patterns have on the quality of our lives. When this awareness provokes an interruption of patterns of avoidance, authentic communication is more likely to follow. Disrupting just one unskillful behavior can interrupt entrenched negative patterns and lead to a series of positive shifts. A mutually shared commitment to new practices can, if successfully implemented, transform even those relationships that have been deeply entrenched in negative patterns.

In addition to creating an agreement with our partner, collaboration with others can give us new ideas regarding specific practices that may support the changes we wish to bring about. This kind of support can help us to trust that real change is possible. Each accomplishment strengthens our motivation to keep up the good work. These wins accumulate over time, and they eventually create the Big Win: a relationship worth protecting and treasuring, where each person's needs are fulfilled, and where resentment and despair have been transformed into harmony and appreciation. All in all, that sounds like a pretty decent trade-off.

Myth 32

Independence is strength, dependence is weakness.

Linda: In the early years of my relationship with Charlie, I was often plagued by a nagging voice inside my head that taunted me with reprimands like: "Why are you so needy? You should be able to fulfill your needs by yourself. You're just a hungry love addict. You should be more self-sufficient. What's wrong with you?!!"

The inside of my mind was not a particularly safe location. It was inhabited frequently by the voice of a powerful and persuasive inner critic who believed that my dependence meant that I was childish, neurotic, weak, and needy. I did eventually manage to recover from those inner critic attacks, although on occasion they still occur. The difference is that nowadays I can fight back. The most effective weapon that I have in my arsenal is my recognition that there is such a thing as a healthy degree of emotional dependence as well as such a thing as unhealthy counter-dependence, which is the tendency to deny vulnerability and the need for emotional support.

We live in a culture that idealizes self-sufficiency. Consequently, many people tend to demonize any degree of dependence and see it as weakness. In order to avoid the judgments of others (and of oneself), many try to conceal any form of interpersonal dependence. Unmet dependency needs don't disappear when they are denied. They migrate to other behaviors, such as drug addiction or workaholism.

Despite our insistence to the contrary, we are essentially, fundamentally, and undeniably interdependent beings. The word *dependence* is defined as "the state of relying on or needing someone or something for aid [or] support." The definition is neutral, but for many, the word *dependency* connotes something negative. In our "me-centered" society, it is a widely held belief that to achieve maturity we must become absolutely autonomous and self-sufficient. If we allow others to become dependent on us, or if we become dependent on others, this is typically viewed as negative or even pathological.

We enter into relationship with others because relating to them enhances our life in some way. None of us is completely independent of the need of others in order to thrive physically, emotionally, and even spiritually. We are dependent upon healthcare providers to stay healthy and to help us heal when we're not; pilots to fly the planes that transport us to faraway places; and chefs to provide us with delicious meals. Healthy dependency or interdependency characterizes all loving relationships. We find ourselves drawn to others who have complementary strengths and character traits, which enable us to create greater wholeness together. To lean on another's strengths is a sign of intelligence rather than weakness.

From time to time, everyone depends on the help of others.

Our friend Seymour says, "Sometimes we push our partner's wheelchair, and sometimes they push ours." This strong image reminds us of the reciprocal nature of relationships. When we fail to acknowledge how much we depend upon the support of others, life becomes more difficult. When we deny our natural dependence due to fear, or to old habituated patterns, we rob ourselves of an opportunity for more ease and pleasure in life. Denying our dependence on others can be just as debilitating as excessive dependence. Both extremes lead to imbalance in our life.

The most successful relationships are those where both partners feel that they are with someone whom they can depend upon. A mutually healthy dependency promotes self-esteem, self-confidence, and ease in life. Agreeing to create an interdependent relationship, we open to the possibility of soothing old wounds, healing dysfunctional family patterns, modeling a successful partnership for our children, and becoming the best that we can each be.

When I look back now on the suffering that I experienced from my belief that I was weak, I feel sad that I was so ignorant for so long. I had bought into the cultural myth of self-sufficiency. I have since come to understand that we all need to hear positive messages about our abilities and strengths, what I call "believing eyes."

When we experience being deeply loved, we begin to feel more comfortable in our own skin. Much of the frantic energy that drives so many of us has to do with running away from ourselves because we've never learned to free ourselves of the negative judgments that we've inherited from our families and others. As we come to be more accepting and to appreciate ourselves, "rushaholism" diminishes and eventually disappears. We can experience the whole spectrum of connectedness, from the deepest intimate bonding with another to the feeling of peaceful tranquillity that often emerges on a solitary retreat.

The myth of independence promotes isolation and loneliness. The degree to which I thrive in my life has to do not only with my feelings of inner security but with the quality of my relationships. There seems to be a growing concern these days that marriage is going out of vogue, that it's not a viable model for contemporary society. That's not how I see it. Marriage for me has been a deeply corrective experience that has enabled me to trust that I can depend on someone to show up with and for me. Charlie has been able to hold my feelings with me without passing judgment, which has been a lifesaver when I have been challenged with my own self-judgments or the judgments of others. Together we have practiced the art of moving back and forth between poles of merger and separateness. It is this ongoing dynamic dance that has allowed me to increasingly embody the fullness of my being.

It is a gift to our partner to acknowledge our reliance upon them and to express our gratitude for their talents, passions, gifts, good sense, and competencies. These are the ways that we honor each other's strengths. One of the gifts that great relationships offer is assistance in facing life's inevitable challenges. We can meet them with confidence, and we can afford to take on challenges that are bigger, grander, and more exciting, resting in the assurance that we are fully supported. Knowing we're not alone can mean the difference between feeling anxious or blessed.

Myth 33

Some people have all the luck.

When it comes to love, luck can and often does play a part for many couples. For instance, your car breaks down and the guy who pulls over to give you a jump start just happens to have recently broken up with his girlfriend. Or you are seated on the plane next to the one person you couldn't take your eyes off of while you were waiting to board.

While luck can play a part in meeting that special person, luck alone will only get you so far. Great partnerships are characterized by love, passion, trust, mutual support, respect, fun, and, of course, great sex. Once you get past the early stage of infatuation, it takes quite a bit more than luck to go the distance and create a truly fulfilling long-term connection. Sometimes, however, when we've gotten lucky in love and managed to meet the right person, we make the mistake of assuming that our good fortune will continue indefinitely. Believing this, we may allow ourselves to become complacent with the expectation that the most important part of the process is handled and now behind us. This could cause us to make the fatal flaw of putting things on cruise control, thinking that the momentum of our mutual love will carry us forever and ever.

Big mistake! Relying on luck can set us up for a huge disappointment. We may envy those couples who seem to be such a good match for each other, but the chances are pretty good that they had to do some serious work to create what they have, or else they are still in the infatuation stage of their romance, or what we see and project onto them doesn't necessarily represent the truth of their relationship. After all, looks can sometimes be deceiving.

The road to mastery in the field of relationships is no different than in any other endeavor in life. The same factors apply: a strong desire and motivation, a willingness to make the necessary sacrifices, a high level of support, and a clear intention to prioritize your purpose. Although the art of creating exceptional relationships requires lots of patience and perseverance, the benefits of our effort reveal themselves early in the process. Also, they don't show up in just our primary partnership, but they show up in all our relationships. Those benefits include a heightened capacity for deep connection and intimacy, enhanced trust and trustworthiness, greater effectiveness in conflict resolution, and a sense of deeper satisfaction and well-being in life.

Like anyone else, I'll gratefully take as much luck as I can get. I just don't want to count on it, since it's one of those elements in life that I can't control. But there are lots of other things in life that I can control, like keeping my word, making my best effort, living in integrity with my true values, and walking my talk. And this is just for starters. Some people believe that the more dedicated you are to fulfilling your commitment, the more luck you get. I don't think that's a myth!

Myth 34

Relationships require a lot of sacrifice.

Joan and Frank had been married for over twenty years and had three children. Frank was a career diplomat, and Joan, like many women of her generation, had dedicated her life to supporting her husband's career. Joan made deep friendships and started projects wherever they lived in the world, but these were always uprooted each time Frank was transferred. When they returned to the United States, Joan decided that it was finally her turn. She enrolled in a local university to pursue a graduate degree and was awarded a full fellowship.

Just before school started, Frank had a massive heart attack, from which he eventually recovered. During one of Joan's visits, she reassured him that her support would continue as long as he needed it. Joan said, "Frank, don't worry, I'll stay right here by your side. I've changed my mind about graduate school. That's not important anymore. I'll stay home and take care of you."

Frank's response was not what Joan expected. With a massive effort, he heaved himself up to a near sitting position and said, "Joan, you will do no such thing. You must go to school... you must!" In that moment, Joan felt like she literally had no choice. "Okay, okay," Joan said. "I'll go to school."

After spending a month in the hospital, Frank went home to continue his recovery, and Joan began her graduate program. It was a turning point in both of their lives. Frank was relieved of his need to continually strive and achieve, and Joan was finally able to fulfill her ambition to be something more than a wife and mother.

This vignette illuminates an important aspect of all great relationships, which is that they *do* require some degree of personal sacrifice. The question is how much. And is the sacrifice mutual? In Joan and Frank's case, Frank felt strongly that it was now his turn to support Joan in the fulfillment of her life dream. His clarity was so strong that it penetrated through Joan's attachment to her role of "sacrificer in chief." The new balance profoundly enhanced their individual lives as well as their marriage. Such radical changes are sometimes necessary in order to promote the growth of a relationship toward higher levels of fulfillment and greater achievements. What Joan saw as a sacrifice on Frank's part, he saw as a gift to her, himself, and their marriage. Frank said, "I was grateful for the opportunity to give back to Joan a small portion of the support that she had given to me over the years."

Being committed to another's well-being is the basis of a cycle of mutual generosity that creates an ongoing, self-reinforcing loop that deepens and becomes more enriching over time. The most successful couples don't "give to get," but rather they give their care and support to each other from a well that is already full. They generally don't see themselves as being unselfish or especially considerate; they simply act in response to a perceived need. They trust that their own lives will be enhanced rather than diminished as a result of their attention to their partner. Consequently, there is no sense of "sacrifice" in the usual understanding of this term. These couples engage in "enlightened self-interest," which is another way to say, "What goes around comes around." Enlightened self-interest means that everybody wins.

When each partner's fulfillment becomes a high priority to both people, other personal preferences naturally become subordinate. Feelings of sacrifice dissolve because we are not giving up anything that we really need, and we are gaining the gratification that comes from supporting a loved one. Getting "my way" becomes much less of a priority because getting "our way" becomes what we both really want.

Each person still has their preferences; these don't go away. But they are only preferences. Fulfilling them isn't urgent. Partners are finally relieved of the need to keep score, since the object of the game is no longer to make sure that each person gets their share. Rather, the couple cocreates as much mutual happiness as possible.

Enlightened self-interest, which arises from a sense of wholeness, sufficiency, and love, is different from codependency, which arises out of feelings of fear, scarcity, and insufficiency. In a codependent relationship, one partner may stretch into the other's world, following their lead, trying to please them because they are fearful that if they don't, unpleasant repercussions will occur. Love, rather than fearfulness, motivates the acts of generosity that spring from enlightened self-interest.

The shadow side of enlightened self-interest is that when

our partner feels pain, sadness, or disappointment, we are so close to them that we too suffer. It's a package plan. We can't experience the joy of giving and receiving without also experiencing the suffering that is inherent in life. Many people avoid closeness out of a desire to avoid feeling their partner's suffering. Unfortunately, you can't have one without the other.

When we make our partner's needs as important, but not more or less important, than our own, we internalize the experience of enlightened self-interest. Feeling the pain of our partner is part of the price we pay to share their joy. This process isn't limited to one person. You can apply it to anyone, or everyone, in your life! Imagine what life would be like if you brought enlightened self-interest into all your relationships. That might seem unrealistic, but it's also possibly the most practical thing that you could ever do!

Myth 35

Play is for kids.

As self-help books constantly remind us, great relationships require work. But there is a counterpart to work that is, in our estimation, at least as important. That would be "play." You don't hear much about the need for play in the creation of an optimal relationship. This is unfortunate, since it reinforces the idea that relationships aren't much fun. Sure, relationships aren't fun-filled all the time, but play is an essential aspect of relationship-building. At times, play helps us remember *why* we chose our partner in the first place, and play helps provide us with the motivation to hang in there when work *is* required. In fact, one of the best ways for us to keep that motivation alive and healthy, whether we're in the early stages of a relationship or after several decades of marriage, is to prioritize play.

Play isn't something that responsible people outgrow once they reach adulthood. In *Play: How It Shapes the Brain, Opens the Imagination, and Invigorates the Soul*, Stuart Brown — the founder and director of the National Institute for Play in Carmel, California — makes the claim that play is intrinsic to our nature and is an essential ingredient for all well-balanced lives and relationships, regardless of our age.

Brown defines play as activities that are done simply for the pleasure of doing them, rather than as a means to an end, like winning or gaining recognition. Play feels good; it's fun and often exciting. We become more fully present when engaged in play and less self-conscious. Play also opens us to experiencing things in new ways that can allow for greater creativity, chance, spontaneity, and serendipity. Play isn't so much a particular activity as an attitude that we bring to whatever we're doing. It's an attitude of nonattachment to a specific outcome and of being present and engaged in our current experience. It's the joy of doing something for its own sake.

When our closest relationships are dominated by internalized expectations and "shoulds," they lose flexibility. Play is the antidote to the feeling of being constrained within a relationship. At times, we may feel obliged to follow established rules, to please and accommodate others, and to make efficient use of our time, and we may feel oppressed by a vague sense of guilt when we fail to fulfill any of the "shoulds" in our relationship. Play liberates us from the feeling of being encumbered by the many explicit and implicit social and interpersonal expectations that we experience daily.

Play is its own reward, its own reason for being. Humans, like all members of the animal kingdom, play from our earliest moments, and despite cultural beliefs, we never outgrow the need for play. We never stop experiencing its benefits throughout our lives. The biggest obstacle to keeping play alive isn't a lack of money or time, nor is it the responsibilities that we have elected to assume, or our age, or even our physical condition. We can bring a playful attitude to any situation. The resistance that many of us experience to becoming more playful isn't external; it's internal. It's our belief that adulthood is serious business, except for those socially sanctioned events when we are allowed to loosen the grip of our internalized self-expectations. But these rare and fleeting moments of playfulness, particularly if they are dependent upon alcohol or drugs, aren't sufficient to experience the benefits that more sustained playfulness provides. Giving ourselves more permission to integrate a playful spirit into our relationships requires the willingness to appear foolish, immature, and even irresponsible. It risks being accused of "not acting your age," which really translates as, "You're having too much fun!"

For many, the fear of being perceived in these ways or judged negatively by our partner prevents us from taking ourselves less seriously. Play doesn't mean avoiding the inevitable difficulties and complexities of the modern world, but rather engaging them and meeting these challenges with a more playful spirit. In particular, bringing more playfulness into our relationships can actually be one of the most responsible things that we can do. Many people try to extend adolescence in an attempt to delay the onset of adulthood and all its stress and responsibilities. Instead, we can become adults while also continuing to play, have fun, be curious, and keep learning.

Play is essentially interpersonal; it almost always involves other people. Because it is an attitude, rather than a specific behavior, it can be brought into nearly any activity. When our primary intention is to experience pleasure or fun, our objective isn't simply getting the job done, but creating a certain experience, whether we are dancing, dishwashing, cleaning the garage, taking a walk, or cooking a meal. As we integrate these dual intentions into our lives, the line between work and play becomes increasingly blurred. And that's a good thing.

When we look for opportunities to bring play into our lives, we find that we don't have to add a lot of new activities. We simply bring this attitude into what we are already doing. Increased enjoyment is a by-product of that intention. Relationships thrive when we play more, because play is a powerful de-stressor, and stress is a major source of relationship difficulties.

If you think that you're not the "playful type," think again. Even the most serious person can embody an attitude of play. Spend more time with friends you may feel are "immature" or "insufficiently responsible." You may have something to learn from them. And vice versa.

In *Still Life With Woodpecker*, Tom Robbins reminds us, "It's never too late to have a happy childhood." Whatever your age, get out there and put a little play in your heart.

Myth 36

It's possible to divorce-proof your marriage.

Sometimes couples are more at risk when things are going well than when they are going through relationship challenges. When there is trouble, there is a strong motivation to bring attentive concern to the relationship and to be more awake and proactive around healing and restoring whatever is broken. We know that we have to do something. But the need to care for a relationship isn't limited to times of breakdown. It's an ongoing process.

When things are going well, we tend to assume they will continue to go well. It doesn't seem like there is much need to attend to the relationship. We are apt to go on cruise control out of the expectation that a high level of attention is no longer required. This attitude has led to disastrous outcomes for many couples. More couples lose their relationships because of a slow process of drifting apart, boredom, and neglect than from a dramatic trauma.

No marriage, no matter how good, is divorce-proof. To

assume yours is can lull you into a false sense of security, and you run the risk of becoming less attentive to each other. Even the best relationships are vulnerable to life's many possible pitfalls. Complacency is dangerous. Even the best relationships can be subject to deterioration, so remain vigilant about providing ongoing care of yours.

We have worked with many people who have been surprised when their partner has reported feeling unhappy or that they wanted to separate. These people felt that they were broadsided out of nowhere. However, in many of these situations, they had let their attentiveness to the relationship slip. They didn't think constant attention was necessary. Believing that you can afford to put your relationship on cruise control is dangerous.

Strengthening your shared commitment and practicing mutual generosity, compassion, honesty, kindness, and respect are all ways of maximizing the likelihood not only of staying together but of experiencing greater mutual fulfillment. When couples become complacent, they often fail to embody these qualities and practices consistently.

It's great when things are going well, but don't stop doing the things that have enabled you to thrive. Don't be lulled into a false sense of security. Keep doing those things that allow your relationship to flourish. Stay awake, and your relationship can build a foundation that can sustain you both for the rest of your lives.

Myth 37

Once I attract my ideal mate, my life will be perfect.

Lately there's been a lot of talk about the "law of attraction." Simply put, this refers to the idea that by intensely focusing your attention on what you want and keeping "negative" thoughts — those related to fear, anger, doubt, guilt, and so on — out of your consciousness, you will draw into your life whatever it is that you truly desire. This philosophy is somewhat simplistic, particularly when it comes to relationships. While it certainly is beneficial to avoid getting ensnared in the trap of obsessive negative thinking, positive thoughts are generally not enough to bring about a desired outcome.

Naturally, the idea that your positive thoughts can attract the relationship of your dreams is quite attractive. So is the idea that a website or dating service might be able to match two strangers who would be perfect for each other. However, meeting someone we connect with isn't really the hardest part. The fly in the ointment, to use a somewhat unattractive metaphor, is that once we attract a partner, we have to sustain the relationship.

The dictionary defines the word *sustain* as meaning "to give support to, to keep up the vitality or courage of." Relationships require support and vitality in order to thrive. And as anyone who has successfully navigated their way through the sometimes treacherous waters of committed partnership knows, it takes courage as well, lots of it. This territory can be dangerous, especially when we have been hurt in past relationships and want to protect ourselves from future pain, or when we want to avoid the possibility of loss or disappointment. It takes a lot of work and practice to learn how to build healthy relationships, and we often end up having to learn about it on the job.

The problem with focusing primarily or exclusively on attracting a partner and neglecting this skill-building is that, once we successfully attract that special someone who really lights up our life, we have to navigate the sometimes choppy waters of any committed partnership. If we don't know how, we're likely to run aground on the rocks, and we will have to look all over again for someone new to attract. We need to focus on learning the fine art of managing any relationship's inevitable challenges, so that we develop the necessary tools and know how to use them when we need them.

Getting clear about the kind of person that you want to share your life with is, of course, an essential prerequisite to finding the partner of your dreams. By all means identify the type of person you'd like to attract. But don't stop there. The next stage of the game is working together to lay a foundation. That will require more than visualizing and affirming all the positive things that you want to experience with your beloved.

It also involves acknowledging your shadow side, or the less-attractive qualities that you both possess. It means having honest conversations about your fears, needs, hopes, strengths, weaknesses, and vision. It involves doing the groundwork that provides the kind of emotional security that you both need in order to feel safe enough to reveal the deep truths that you each hold. It involves skillfully dealing with conflict management and communication. Admittedly, listening without judgment and speaking without defensiveness is easier said than done, but with practice and the willingness to share responsibility, you and your mate can create the partnership of your dreams.

Myth 38

When it comes to relationships, security is always better.

Great relationships are not just about comfort and security. This isn't news to anyone who has been married for a while or anyone who has ever been in a stagnant relationship. Still, we all want to feel safe in our relationships, and we want to minimize risks, so we often make predictability, security, comfort, and stability our main priority. Cocreating a protective structure is a good thing. But too much of a good thing can be a bad thing. It can result in undesirable consequences, such as boredom, restlessness, resentment, depression, acting out (as in affairs), and the flatlining of intimacy.

The desire for physical, financial, and emotional security is not misguided, far from it, but the devil is in the details, as it were. In particular, the issue is how highly two partners prioritize the commitment to or need for security.

Identifying this can be a tricky process, since many of the agreements that couples make are implicit, unspoken, and even unrecognized. We all have our own "set points" for what we find to be comfortable levels of risk and security. It's not uncommon for a person with a lower threshold for risk to be in a relationship with someone with a relatively higher one. The dynamic tension of such a match can be a source of distress, depending upon the difference in each partner's comfort levels and their respective skills in dealing with differences. Yet regardless of the differences, all couples have an (unspoken) agreed-upon level of comfort that they negotiate on an ongoing basis. Each partner offers balance on the risk/security continuum.

When the relationship is unbalanced, it can lead to potentially damaging consequences. Excessive ballast can keep risk so low that there's insufficient challenge, play, change, or spontaneity, and insufficient grounding can expose the couple to too much financial, emotional, physical, or material risk. The challenge when relational imbalance occurs is not to take an either/or, "my way or the highway" stance. Rather, identify the needs of the relationship as opposed to focusing on accommodating either partner.

This requires compromise, which doesn't mean each partner has to give in to the other or give up their preferences. It's about seeing the big picture and recognizing that there will be times that the risk-tolerant person will have to accommodate the risk-averse person, and vice versa. The operative word is *balance*, not necessarily *fair* or *equal*. It's the relationship itself that both partners are deferring to, not necessarily each other.

When both partners acknowledge the need to have a balanced set point that is healthy and acceptable to each person, the adjustments become much easier and quicker to recognize and implement.

Rather than seeking to make the larger and more invasive

macro-adjustments, which are required when the system has become destabilized, we are more attuned to the need for on-going monitoring to create balance. We make more frequent but also subtler and minimally invasive "micro-corrections" to the system.

To use another analogy, all relationships require roots *and* wings. Sometimes each partner is sufficiently balanced internally and can recognize and respond to whatever the needs of the moment happen to be. More often than not, we are in relationship with someone whose personal set point is slanted in one direction or the other. Of course, each partner will have their own (usually complementary) bias. The challenge in these situations is to resist the temptation, strong as it might be, to view ourselves as having the "correct" perspective and our partner as needing to conform to our point of view.

It can make it a little easier to detach from this view when we think about how things might be if we both were operating from the same orientation. Recognizing our own tendency (toward greater risk or greater security) can be very helpful in enabling us to let go of the notion that we are right and the other is wrong. From our experience, this is possible and well worth the investment of time, energy, and effort that is required to develop this inner flexibility.

When this degree of flexibility is embodied by each partner, the set point and tolerance level will naturally rise to a higher level as a result of the increased feelings of trust, support, and mutual understanding.

Don't wait until the potentially damaging symptoms of an imbalance in the risk/security continuum manifest themselves. Both excessive risks as well as insufficient stimulation can be relationship-killers. Get on top of things and stay on top of them; frequently review how things are going for you, your partner, and your relationship. Identify and negotiate the changes that are needed and take actions that you both feel will readjust the balance. Then get in the habit of doing that on an ongoing basis. You'll be amazed what a difference this will make. We guarantee it!

Myth 39

Married couples don't date.

Despite the fact that it's been all over the media for years — that it is important to date your mate — large numbers of couples still believe that dating is just for those who are in the courtship stage of their relationship. Over time, many married couples eventually stop dating altogether, and some rationalize this by claiming they don't have enough time. This is a convenient way to avoid being proactive in keeping love alive in a long-term relationship.

Feelings of attraction, desire, or sexual excitement tend to dwindle under these circumstances, but this isn't inevitable. It happens because these qualities aren't being attended to. Consequently, the future may look bleak and uninspiring. This expectation can be the prelude to a downward trajectory. Of course, feelings of desire can wax and wane for lots of reasons, but it is possible to strengthen the substance of your relationship in a way that minimizes low periods and diminishes their frequency. What it takes is a commitment to infuse your life with more fun and pleasure, and to keep your relationship fresh, passionate, and exciting, whether you're twenty or ninety.

After a few years of married life, it's easy to slip into being roommates, business partners, and co-parents. As important as these roles are, if our relationship becomes defined by them, our role as lovers can be squeezed out.

In most relationships, one partner tends to place a higher value on romance than the other. The person who is the advocate for keeping romance alive will be more likely to notice when it is fading. Consequently, this partner can introduce corrections to bring more closeness and playfulness. This is not to imply that he or she has the sole responsibility for keeping an eye on things, but rather because of this awareness, that partner is more capable of noticing and influencing the need for connection.

What are some of the myriad ways to bring more of this spirit into a relationship? Go out on a date. Dates aren't just for young lovers; they work magic for anyone, no matter how long a couple has been together. Getting away from home provides a change of scenery and enlivens things for both partners.

Staying home for a date can be fun, too. You can have a romantic dinner by candlelight. Consider making date night a regular feature of your relationship. Dates don't have to be limited to a few hours together on an occasional evening; they can be an entire day, a weekend, or even longer. Nor are honeymoons (without the kids, of course) just for the newly married. Taking one every year is not too much. We know lots of people, including ourselves, who have made a tradition of this practice.

Taking time to honor the intimacy component of your

partnership can become habit-forming. Try some of these, and add your own creative touches to keep romance alive.

1. Designate what we refer to as "sacred time," and create a tech-free zone that will ensure that there will be *no* interruptions. Then, enjoy.

2. Some delightful ways of spending an evening together don't cost anything. Getting into the tub with each other, with candlelight, of course, followed by more candlelight in the bedroom is a sure way to enhance the spirit of romance.

3. Take turns being in service to each other. You can bathe each other and wash each other's hair or take turns shaving each other.

4. Agree beforehand to feed each other an entire meal. We know a number of couples that have done this in restaurants, often to the surprise of other diners. Sit across the corner of the table so you can be close to each other. Feeding each other slows down the rate at which you eat. This is also a good way to lose weight, since generally, the slower we eat, the less we eat.

5. Spend time being connected through your eyes only, without the need to exchange words. While this may seem a bit awkward at first, after a few minutes you'll begin to settle in, and you may experience some surprisingly delightful feelings.

6. After dinner you can listen to music together, and you might even dance. If you'd prefer privacy, try dancing with your partner in your own living room or bedroom. Another big advantage of dancing in your own home is that you can take

your clothes off. You'll know for sure that you are not roommates or business partners when you're dancing nude!

7. Massage is another great way to keep romance alive. You don't need a massage table or fancy scented massage oils. Just take the cooking oil down from the kitchen shelf, and lay down a towel on the bed or floor. And you don't have to be a professionally trained masseuse or masseur to bring a loving touch.

8. Reading love poems to each other brings sweetness. If you enjoy the exotic, consider poetry by Rumi, Hafiz, or Kabir.

9. Love notes stuck in books, under plates and pillows, and in the underwear drawer are sure to draw smiles of appreciation.

10. Last, but not least, is romantic talk. It needs to be sincere, intimate, and full of feeling from the heart. These emotional interchanges are the main meal. Sex is the dessert, and it's nonfattening.

Taking time out of our busy lives to make sure that the intimate aspects of our relationship are thriving works wonders for the partnership and our lives as a whole. Trying something new can promote more thrills and excitement than anxiety if we are mindful about the ways in which we approach change.

We can rest assured that the lovers' aspect of our relationship is thriving when we're enjoying the art of bringing pleasure to each other. Plus, we receive the added benefit of all those health-enhancing hormones running through our body that promote happiness and well-being.

Mmmmmmm, good!

Myth 40

Good relationships require more effort than they're worth.

I f you are one of the people who believe this, you are not alone. This myth can be especially compelling because (A) it is true that creating a truly great relationship usually *does* take some hard work; (B) it's a convenient justification to settle for something mediocre and not even bother trying to create a great relationship; and (C) there's a whole lot of agreement in the world that this assertion is true.

Yes, relationships require not only a significant amount of effort but also the willingness to endure experiencing emotions that we usually want to avoid or deny — like helplessness, anger, confusion, shame, frustration, fear, despair, and loneliness. Yes, loneliness, because even those in committed partnerships can get lonely.

But what is just as true is that the periods of hard work and difficult times are not permanent. They are temporary. Like the Buddhists say, "This too shall pass." And they do pass as we become more skilled and experienced in the art of relationship-building and as we integrate the skills that this process challenges us to master. Those practices involve (among other things) committed listening, letting go of control, cultivating vulnerability, overcoming resistance to change, honesty, and focusing on your own work rather than trying to control your partner. As with mastering any new skill, it takes a lot to hang in there and muddle through the demanding times. The effort required is often great and the challenge can be daunting. It's understandable that many people tend to feel discouraged about the prospect of spending the rest of their lives "working on their relationship."

Relationships, many think, should not have to be this hard. Well, that's true. They shouldn't be endlessly difficult. And they aren't. As a great many couples have discovered, doing the hard work is rewarded by better partnerships that don't feel like work. As we discovered in researching our book *Secrets of Great Marriages*, while most couples have experienced varying degrees of difficulty, after they make it "over the hump," the need for ongoing effort diminishes and the amount of energy required to sustain the relationship is greatly reduced. Furthermore, the experience of nurturing the relationship no longer feels like an ordeal, but rather, it becomes a labor of love that feels like a gift, a joyful opportunity that is now characterized by feelings of gratitude and appreciation.

This characterization may seem unrealistic or Pollyanna-ish to some. But anyone who has successfully transitioned to the more advanced stages of partnership knows it is not only realistic but unquestionably attainable. With trust, perseverance, and hard work, any couple can reach the "gold" that committed partnerships offer. Perseverance is the willingness to continue making the necessary effort to confront any challenges. Trust is the confidence that there is light at the end of the tunnel, whether we can currently see it or not.

Cultivating any new skill, such as playing a musical instrument, learning a foreign language, or mastering a particular sport or game, requires knowledge, diligence, and practice. Developing the skill of effective relating is no different, even though it's easy to forget that most of us are, to varying degrees, relatively unschooled in this arena.

Because we may not think of relationships as something that you need to develop skills for, it's easy to forget that this process is no different than the development of other competencies. Many of us believe that if we feel love and affection for someone, then the relationship should just "naturally" thrive. While it may be natural, most of us have developed some pretty unskillful practices in our attempts to fulfill our needs. Yet while loving another person isn't enough to ensure a blissful future together, what is true is that we do have the ability to participate in ways that strongly influence the degree to which our relationships thrive.

The amount of time that we spend in the early stages of this process and the slope of our learning curve have to do with our willingness and ability to learn the lessons that relationships continually provide. These lessons are about honesty, nonattachment, joyfulness, acceptance, responsibility, commitment, compassion, integrity, gratitude, and courage. The more dedicated we are to developing these and other qualities, the more quickly we will internalize the competencies that good relationships require. As we integrate these abilities, replacing old defensive habits with new, more effective practices, the work becomes more effortless. We naturally begin doing the things that work and let go of habitual responses that no longer serve us. Of course, this takes time, and the process is gradual, but if you can stick with it, the result is not only worth the effort, it's beyond what most of us ever thought possible. And that's the truth.

Afterword

The ability to distinguish fact from fiction is essential in any undertaking that requires skill, discernment, intelligence, commitment, and courage. The art and science of creating great relationships requires all of these and more. In this book our primary focus has been on the untrue, or at least unproven, commonly held beliefs about love, particularly within the context of committed romantic partnerships. The ability to make this distinction is essential for creating a fulfilling relationship, but it's equally valuable to get information from "the trenches," that is, the experience of those who have been there and are still there, who have made the mistakes, stepped on the land mines, shed the tears, and come through the process scathed but wiser.

These are the survivors of the ordeals and delights that come with the territory of truly fulfilling relationships. Not only have they lived to tell about it, but they are our much-needed guides for creating a twenty-first-century paradigm for relationships.

We live in a world in which staying together for the sake of children, financial security, and social pressures is no longer enough to sustain a partnership. It is important to discover our goals and to create connections that are mutually fulfilling, life-enriching, soul-nourishing, and meaningful to everyone involved, children as well as adults.

Prior to the twentieth century, and for most of human history, the primary purpose of marriage was to provide physical and material sustenance for individuals, couples, families, and larger groups, identified by ethnicity, regional identification, and religious or spiritual affiliation. Only within the past two or three generations has another goal been added to this list. That is, in addition to fulfilling our physical, material, and financial needs, a relationship is expected to also fulfill our desire to experience meaning, purpose, and emotional and spiritual fulfillment. A tall order indeed.

One of the myths that many have bought into is that with the right conditions, the right partner, and the right amount of love, knowledge, money, and effort, fulfilling the dream of a committed partnership should be easy — or at least easier than it seems to be. There is a tendency to underestimate the magnitude of this challenge within the larger context of today's world. People rely on widely accepted cultural beliefs as "shortcuts" to answer difficult relationship concerns rather than investigating things for themselves. While it's understandable that shortcuts are attractive, relying on them can lead to disappointment when they fail to fulfill our expectations or lead us astray.

Stripping away our illusions about love can be a painful

process, since it confronts us with the reality that we can't trust the maps we have created or inherited. Yet within this realization are the seeds for fulfilling our dreams. We (not so) simply need to find the willingness to engage the process of discovery and understand with the "beginner's mind" of a child rather than the "knowing mind" of the expert adult. To do so is to embody a level of vulnerability that can be unsettling. For many, it's an acquired taste, much like appreciating an exotic culinary delicacy.

Our intention in writing this book has been not only to refute forty widely held myths about love but to urge you to engage in the process of distinguishing what you believe from that which is factually true, and to cultivate the courage and discernment to stand outside of the "security" of unproven but commonly held beliefs.

While embracing an idea that is shared by many people can be comforting, sheer numbers don't necessarily make something true. By the same token, our claim that the forty beliefs in this book are actually myths doesn't prove that they are untrue. We only invite you to consider that they may be. In so doing, you will be in a better position to determine what is worth taking seriously and what you can use as a guideline to help you find greater fulfillment in all your relationships.

In closing, we'd like to leave you with a few of the key points that we have learned from our personal experience in our forty-seven-year relationship and from the many clients and students with whom we've worked over the past forty years.

Consider that...

- Despite the heightened expectations of our times and the growing list of commitments that compete

with the needs of our relationships, most couples
give less time than ever to the health and well-
being of their connection.

- There *is* an alternative to the apparent dichotomy
between either staying in a bad marriage or getting a divorce. It's called "doing your own work."
- Doing the work can be challenging, in part because
of the universal tendency to be more attentive to
and aware of our partner's flaws and deficiencies
than to our own.
- Creating a great partnership is possible regardless
of one's past experiences in one's family of origin
or in previous relationships.
- Great relationships do require some hard work,
but they are worth considerably more than the effort that it takes to create them.
- Creating a great relationship generally requires
more time, effort, courage, vulnerability, responsibility, and forgiveness than we think it should.
- It takes years to build a foundation of trust and
respect, and moments to destroy it. In most cases,
however, broken trust can be repaired.
- The choice of a love partner is the most important
decision that you'll ever make.
- The greatest gift that you can give your children
is the example of a loving relationship with your
partner.
- It is possible not only to become accepting of differences but to become grateful for them.
- It only takes one person to begin the process of
repairing a damaged relationship, but unless the

other person eventually joins the healing process, the relationship will be destined to fail.

- More relationships end because of neglect and avoidance than because of conflict.
- It takes more courage to be vulnerable than it does to be hostile and aggressive.
- Yelling louder is less likely to persuade your partner to hear what you are saying than keeping your mouth shut and listening to them before you speak.
- Marriage counseling may seem expensive, but compared to divorce it's ridiculously cheap.
- And finally, the amount of joy and fulfillment available in a loving partnership is vastly more than you can even imagine.

Acknowledgments

S peaking of myths, some people still believe the myth that books are written by only the person who is identified as the author. This book is the product of the efforts, energies, and care of many people. Their offerings have included editing skills, administrative and technical assistance, feedback, writing retreat facilities, encouragement, and 24/7 phone support when we needed it. These people include:

Mary Amrita Arden, David Lustig, Kennett and Bob Roberts, Doug Abrams, Lorrine Cararra, and Tiffanie Luna.

Our readers, Claire Bloom, John Robbins, Roberta Valdez, Frannie Field, Rachel Jablon, Naomi Berger, and Chris Matthies.

Our terrific agent, Devra Jacobs.

Special thanks also to our wonderful team at New World Library, especially editors Georgia Hughes, Jeff Campbell, and Kristen Cashman. Also Munro Magruder, Monique Muhlenkamp, and Marc Allen, cofounder, president, and publisher of New World Library.

And thanks to those we have learned from and been supported by over the years, including Stephen and Ondrea Levine, Thich Nhat Hanh, Jack Kornfield, Jiddu Krishnamurti, Harville Hendrix, Gary Chapman, Gay and Kathlyn Hendricks, Marion Woodman, and Robert Bly. We bow to the wisdom that you have passed on to us and countless others.

We also wish to thank the clients, students, and readers we have worked with over the past forty years that we have been in practice and have facilitated seminars and workshops. Your courage and commitment have moved and inspired us to deepen our dedication to continuing to do our own work.

Last, we wish to thank our children and grandchildren — Sarah and her son, Seth; Jesse and his wife, Cassia, and their sons, Ashton and Devin — for providing the inspiration to stretch ourselves beyond the bounds of our personal experience and into a vision of a world in which peace, love, truthfulness, and integrity are the values that prevail and inform the lives of all people. May it be so.

Notes

Page xvii, *"an unproved or false collective belief that is used to justify a social institution"*: *Dictionary.com*, s.v. "myth," accessed October 2015, http://dictionary.reference.com/browse/myth?s=t.

Page xix, *"marked by deep understanding, keen discernment, and a capacity for sound judgment"*: *Merriam-Webster's Collegiate Dictionary*, 11th ed., s.v. "wise."

Page 5, *"When two people are at one in their inmost hearts"*: *The I Ching or Book of Changes*, ed. Richard Wilhelm and Cary Baynes (1967; repr., New York: Bollingen Foundation, 1997), 59.

Page 9, *"He who isn't busy being born is busy dying"*: Bob Dylan, "It's Alright, Ma (I'm Only Bleeding)," *Bringing It All Back Home* (New York: Columbia, 1965).

Page 10, *Marriage, to quote Stephen Levine, is "the ultimate danger sport"*: Stephen Levine and Ondrea Levine, *Embracing the Beloved: Relationship as a Path of Awakening* (New York: Anchor Books, 1996).

Page 55, *"to love another human being is perhaps the most difficult of all our tasks"*: Rainer Maria Rilke, *Letters to a Young Poet*, 2nd ed. (Novato, CA: New World Library, 2000).

Page 88, *"official consignment, as to a prison or mental health facility"*: *American Heritage Dictionary*, s.v. "commitment," accessed October 2015, http://www.yourdictionary.com/commitment#americanheritage.

Page 94, *One of the researchers, Russell Geen, author of the book* Human
    Aggression: Russell Geen, *Human Aggression*, 2nd ed. (Buckingham,
    England: Open University Press, 2001).

Page 107, *"But let there be spaces in your togetherness"*: Kahlil Gibran, *The Prophet*
    (1923; repr., New York: Knopf, 1990), 15–16.

Page 114, *"A failure to confront is a failure to love"*: M. Scott Peck, *The Road
    Less Traveled* (1978; repr., New York: Touchstone, 2003).

Page 122, *Still more surprising is that according to relationship and sexuality expert
    Esther Perel:* Esther Perel, *Mating in Captivity* (New York: Harper
    Perennial, 2007).

Page 128, *"four horsemen of the apocalypse"*: John Gottman, *Why Marriages Suc-
    ceed or Fail* (New York: Simon and Schuster, 1994), 72.

Page 134, *"the state of relying on or needing someone or something for aid [or]
    support"*: Dictionary.com, s.v. "dependence," accessed October 2015,
    http://dictionary.reference.com/browse/dependence?s=t.

Page 144, *Stuart Brown — the founder and director of the National Institute for
    Play*: Stuart Brown, *Play: How It Shapes the Brain, Opens the Imagination,
    and Invigorates the Soul* (New York: Penguin Books, 2009).

Page 147, *Tom Robbins reminds us, "It's never too late to have a happy childhood"*:
    Tom Robbins, *Still Life With Woodpecker* (New York: Bantam Books,
    1980), final page (unnumbered).

About the Authors

L inda Bloom, LCSW, and Charlie Bloom, MSW, have been assisting individuals, couples, and organizations in the process of enhancing the quality of their relationships since 1975. The founders and codirectors of Bloomwork, they have lectured and taught seminars on relationships since 1986 to thousands of people throughout the United States and in overseas locations, including China, Brazil, India, Japan, Indonesia, Denmark, Sweden, and Bangladesh.

They are regular presenters at the Esalen Institute, the Kripalu Center for Yoga & Health, and Rancho La Puerta. They have also served as adjunct faculty members and lecturers at the California Institute of Integral Studies, the Institute of Imaginal Studies, the University of California Berkeley Extension Program, Antioch University, the Omega Institute, John F. Kennedy University, and many other institutions of higher learning. They have been bloggers for several online journals, including the *Huffington Post*, *Psychology Today*, and *Psych Central*.

Charlie and Linda have been married since 1972. They are the parents of grown children and are grandparents. They live in Northern California.

The Blooms welcome your account of your own experiences in learning about love. Let them know if you are willing to include your story in one of their forthcoming books. They are available for counseling and consulting services by phone, and they also offer DVDs and online teleconferencing. To receive their monthly newsletter or to get their workshop schedule or other information about their work, go to their website at www.bloomwork.com, email them at lcbloom@bloomwork.com, or call 831-421-9822.